93

3000 8000
St. Louis Community College

MW00669226

WITHDRAWN

The Psychology of
Adolescent
Satanism

The Psychology of Adolescent Satanism

A Guide for Parents, Counselors, Clergy, and Teachers

Anthony Moriarty

PRAEGER

Westport, Connecticut
London

Copyright Acknowledgment

The author and publisher are grateful for permission to use the following material:

Moriarty, A. R. (1991). Adolescent Satanic cult dabblers: A differential diagnosis. *Journal of Mental Health Counseling, 13*(3), July, 393-404. Copyright © Sage Publications, Inc. Printed by permission of Sage Publications, Inc.

Library of Congress Cataloging-in-Publication Data

Moriarty, Anthony.
    The psychology of adolescent Satanism : a guide for parents,
counselors, clergy, and teachers / Anthony Moriarty.
       p.   cm.
    Includes bibliographical references and indexes.
    ISBN 0–275–94307–0 (alk. paper)
    1. Satanism—Psychological aspects. 2. Teenagers—Religious life.
    3. Teenagers—Mental health. 4. Adolescent psychology.   I. Title.
BF1548.M67   1992
133.4′22′019—dc20   92–12731

British Library Cataloguing in Publication Data is available.

Library of Congress Catalog Card Number: 92–12731
ISBN: 0–275–94307–0

First published in 1992

Praeger Publishers, 88 Post Road West, Westport, CT 06881
An imprint of Greenwood Publishing Group, Inc.

Printed in the United States of America

The paper used in this book complies with the
Permanent Paper Standard issued by the National
Information Standards Organization (Z39.48–1984).

10 9 8 7 6 5 4 3 2 1

Contents

Acknowledgments xi

1. **The Problem** 1

   The Current Marketplace 3
   This Writer's Assumptions 5
   Disclaimers 7
   Witchcraft 7
   Santeria 8
   Voodoo 8
   Multiple Personality Disorders 9
   Multigenerational Cult Families 9
   The Focus of This Book 9

2. **Personality Types of Adolescents Involved in Satanism** 11

   Psychological Implications of Satanism 12
   A Differential Perspective 13
   The Psychopathic Delinquent 13
   The Angry Misfit 15
   The Pseudo-Intellectual 17
   The Suicidal Impulsive 19
   Conclusion 21

3. **Risk Factors Associated with Satanism** 23

   Cultural Factors 23
   Greater Complexity 23

              Decline of Family Anchors   24
              Lack of Adult Role Models   24
              Emotional Unavailability of Parents   25
              Academic Demands   25
              Peer Pressure   26
           Physical Factors   26
              Body Weight   26
              Sleep Habits   27
              Clothing Styles   27
              Frequent Illnesses   27
           Psychological Factors   28
              Perceptual Threat   28
              Rigid Thinking Patterns   28
              Greater Impulsiveness   29
              Lack of Motivation   29
              General Stress Management   30
              Self-Concept   30
              Spontaneous Remission   32
              Diffuse Anger   32
              Elimination of Guilt   33
              Reversal of Feelings   33
              Bonding Changes   33
           Social Factors   34
              Needs for Privacy   34
              Family Routines   34
              Changing Money Habits   35
              Friendship Patterns   35
           Summary   35

4.   **The Satanic Bible**   37

           LaVey's Seven Major Assumptions   39
              Assumption I: Religion and Pleasure Are
              Mutually Exclusive   39
              Assumption II: Man Is Inherently Violent   40
              Assumption III: Bad and Good Are Reversed   41
              Assumption IV: Satanism Is Strength   41
              Assumption V: Satanism Is Now   42
              Assumption VI: Satanism Is Power   42
              Assumption VII: We Must Choose between
              Sex and Religion   43
           Conclusion   44

5.   **Satanism as a Source of Power**   47

           Occult Power Defined   48
           Perceptual Power   49

The Illusion of Power 49
Developmental Aspects of Power 51
Satanism and Power Needs 52
Conclusion 54

6. **The Satan-God Duality** 55

Dualities in Philosophy 55
Dualities and Language 56
Duality and Death 56
The Duality of Good and Evil 57
The Antichrist: Satan 57
The Duality of Heaven and Hell 59
The Exploitation of Dualities 60
Conclusion 62

7. **Rites of Passage** 63

The Role of Ritual 64
Five Purposes of Rituals 66
    Body-Mind Balance 66
    Transcending Fear 67
    Conferring the Father's Role 68
    Prescribing Rules of Conduct 68
    Acceptance of Death 69
Adolescence: The Missing Ritual 69
Countercultural Rituals 71
Toward a Solution 74

8. **Parent Styles: The Beginning** 77

Parallel Lifestyles 78
Parental Distortions 79
Meeting the Wrong Needs 79
Denial of Problems 79
Rights Preceding Responsibilities 80
Parental Emotional Issues 80
Some Solutions 81
    Independence Training 81
    Limit Setting 84
    Double Binds 85
    Praise 86
    Redirecting Inappropriate Behavior 87
    Responding to Feeling 88
    Self-Disclosure 89
    Role Models 90
    Punishment 91
    Parent Problems 92
Summary 93

 9.   **Communicating Effectively**   95

       Why Communication Is Important   96
       Barrier I: Parallel Communication   97
       Barrier II: Missed Attribution   98
       Barrier III: Perspectives on Forever   98
       Barrier IV: Hidden Anxieties   100
       Barrier V: Vague Messages   100
       Communicating during Crisis Situations   101
            Ownership   102
            Moderate Exposure   103
            Giving Responsibility   103
            Role Models   103
            Family Rituals   104
            Quality Time   104
            Humor   105
       Communicating with Adolescents Involved in Satanism   105
            Critical Thinking Skills   105
            Knowledge as Power   107
            Objective Questioning   107
            Common Ground   108
       Summary   110

10.   **Satanism and Suicide**   111

       The Epidemic of Suicide   112
       General Factors Related to Suicide   112
            The Complexity of Adolescent Life   112
            The Loss of Anchors   113
            Parental Unavailability   113
            Altered Time Perspective   114
            Peer Conflicts   114
            Impulsive Sexuality   115
       Psychological Factors Related to Suicide   116
            Self-Esteem   116
            Learned Helplessness   116
            The Loss of the Future   117
            The Perception of Loss   117
            Free-Floating Anger   118
       Religion and Suicide   119
       The Link between Satanism and Suicide: Drugs   120
       The Case of Religious Cults   121
       Suicide and Satan: The Double Draw   122
       Making Sense of Suicide   123
       Suicidal Thinking   125
       Conclusion   126

11. Summary   127

    Personal Empowerment   127
    Love   128
    An Accurate Assessment of Evil   129
    Religion   130
    Drug and Alcohol Use   131
    Privacy   132
    Knowledge   132
    Helping Others   132
    Communication   133
    Role Models   133
    Conclusion   134

References   135

Author Index   141

Subject Index   145

Acknowledgments

The primary focus of this book is prevention and early intervention. It argues that the roots of vulnerability to the influence of Satanism are a long time in the making. It also maintains that Satanic involvement is preventable. As a result, parents and others who work with children need to know how these patterns of vulnerability develop. This book is dedicated to all of us who are charged with the enormous responsibility of helping children grow into responsible adults.

It is also presumptious to assume this work was done in isolation. The support of my wife, Allenda, and my daughters, Erin and Meghan, has been invaluable. They have shown great patience while I spent time writing and gathering information for this book.

Finally, the nuts and bolts of writing a book involve a lot of talents, many of which I do not possess. Paul Macirowski, my editor, has shown the insight and ability to keep me on task. Kathy Fleming, Gloria Roesing, Denise Manning, and Kelly May were able to type a manuscript that made no sense at times. A special debt of gratitude is owed Jennifer Yos, whose relentless editing, critiquing, and correcting of my writing make the unthinkable not only thinkable but readable. Finally, thanks to Cousin Kate and the Sisters of Mercy. Once again, they knew the right thing and did it.

The Psychology of
Adolescent
Satanism

1

The Problem

Satanism became an area of professional interest for me out of necessity. The first time an adolescent revealed his Satanic beliefs to me, I was in for a revelation I was totally unprepared to address. My therapeutic relationship with this young man, and subsequently others, revealed a convoluted system of occult beliefs that powerfully affected all aspects of his personal identity. The transformation of his identity was nowhere more evident than in the feeling of power he exuded. This was a complete reversal of the way he appeared to act before his Satanic involvement. He fully believed that he was now a person of great power who held the fate of others in his hands. The embeddedness of these beliefs and their pervasive impact were most striking to me. Whether this was true or not was insignificant. The fact that this perception of power obtained for him this sense of conviction, poise, and persuasion among his peers made all the difference in the world to him. He was totally immune to self-doubt, fear, or guilt. Consequently, there was no incentive to change. Some people would say he sold his soul to the devil. I realized that adolescent Satanism defined a new set of therapeutic issues for a counselor or any other adult committed to helping young people.

Getting the problems of this young man into focus for therapy was a frustrating job. This involvement in Satanism, it seemed, changed all the rules. The common underlying emotions of fear, guilt, and anxiety that drive so many human problems were no longer valid guides for understanding. My traditional modes of thinking about adolescents no longer made sense. What might have otherwise been a commonly observed pattern of oppositional acting-out behavior was now something very different.

After discussing the referral of this young man with a local school counselor, I expected to meet a frustrated, impulsive, and angry young man, of whom I have seen many in fifteen years as a clinical psychologist. Adolescents often are alike in their feelings of alienation, low self-esteem, and anger toward the world. This pattern of troubles is almost always rooted in an intense feeling of helplessness that is denied.

Not so with this young Satanist. He presented himself with a sense of power and control that was eerie. He controlled the venting of his anger with the accuracy of a marksman. His targets were those in authority, most notably his parents. He knew exactly what he was doing. He also praised Satan for giving him this new lease on life. He reveled in this power. He constructed a worldview around the dichotomy of the forces of evil against the forces of good, convinced that evil would prevail. He practiced rituals that he thought gave him more power. His authority was *The Satanic Bible*. He had an entirely new view of suicide, claiming it could lead him to a position of enormous power. This kid was really different.

This pattern of behavior and its underlying motivational systems did not fit anything I had previously seen or read about. All of my assumptions about adolescent emotional problems were so challenged by this young man that I was left with little traditional framework to deal with him. Feeling uncomfortable and frustrated by this, I turned to the growing collection of work by experts in my professional library. For once, they were of little help. Virtually nothing has been written in this area for the professional.

Still in need of some understanding, I looked to the popular literature on Satanism and the general area of occultism that seems to occupy increasing shelf space at the local bookstore. I found a number of books on Satanism, most of which would frighten the bejesus out of anyone. These were of little help since they focused primarily on the "what" question. They made little effort to delve into the reasons why young people find Satanism so attractive. Those that tried to address the "why" question did so with such a narrow focus they were of meager assistance. Fundamentalist Christian beliefs are helpful in some cases, but not this one. Too often, it seems, these religious arguments are constructed dualistically and are difficult to apply to the problem of Satanism. Either you are with us, they argue, or you are against us and, therefore, doing the work of the devil. Also of little value was the emotional rant about music or the much maligned Dungeons and Dragons.

To make matters worse, the frustration and tinge of fear I first experienced with this young man paled in comparison with the response of his parents. They were utterly bewildered and really scared. Suddenly they were the bad guys and on the defensive. They clung more tenaciously to their traditional family values and religious beliefs. In so doing, however, they more fully embodied a representation of the antithesis of Satan, giving this young man a more focused opportunity to reject their traditional values. No book could explain to them what was going on. Those available would only generate more fear. The problem of understanding Satanism is greatly exacerbated by fear. It is a destructive emotion to anyone interested in understanding why Satanism is of such interest to young people.

This book puts fear aside and provides an objective look at the causes of Satanism and how we may unintentionally increase an adolescent's vulnerability to Satanic beliefs. Tracing the roots of vulnerability to Satanism involves a quest through philosophy, anthropology, religion, psychology, and communication. The causes of Satanism are multidimensional. So, too, are the ways it can be viewed and addressed. First, we will briefly summarize the available books on this subject.

THE CURRENT MARKETPLACE

Many books on cults have found their way to bookstore shelves. Some of these books describe the problems of Satanism, its impact on society, and the young people who are affected by this phenomenon. Not all have done so with objectivity or accuracy, however.

Lurid descriptions of violence and mayhem committed by young people are attributed to the work of Satan. St. Clair's *Say You Love Satan* (1987), for example, chronicles the sadistic murder of a teenager, leading the reader to believe that Satanism was the cause of this tragedy. He presumes that Satanism caused this mayhem rather than thinking that the propensity for such violence preceded the Satanic ideas. Other books, such as Lyons's *Satan Wants You: The Cult of Devil Worship in North America* (1988), provide titillating tales that fascinate curious readers and entice them to seek more information about Satanism. Weaving a variety of individual opinions about occult criminal activity into one Satanic theme, Kahaner (1988) attempts to show ''the far-reaching breadth of this type of crime" (p. viii). The uninformed and naive reader is left to believe that Satanism is a problem of epidemic proportion in our society.

Still others have badly confused Satanism with evil in general, leading their readers to an unsubstantiated conclusion that all acts of evil are orchestrated by Satan himself, who is working to undermine all goodness, especially as it is expressed through organized religion. Raschke (1990) and Johnston (1989) present a national conspiracy theory of Satanism by proposing such a creative and broad definition of Satanism that it includes a variety of evil doings. Johnston attributes sexual perversion, violence, drugs, psychic suicide, and spiritual self-destruction to Satanism (1989, pp. 260–261). Virtually anything he disagrees with is Satanic. This is a dangerous step toward religious totalitarianism.

These conspiracy proponents make the job of eradicating evil more complicated and difficult. Since Satan provokes fear and other intense negative emotions in the majority of people, they are left to cope with irrational fear rather than to address an objective challenge. It becomes an emotional issue, difficult to address productively.

Conspiracy proponents employ scare tactics. With no attention to evidence or logic, they create an overwhelming scenario for the uninformed reader who is attempting to learn about Satanism. They tell of sinister covens of Satanists snatching up babies and torturing, killing, and eating them in grisly ritualistic homage to Satan. These tales of terror are given further credence by the distribution of the Satanic calendar, which, by their interpretation, calls for the sacrifice of human life on various holidays throughout the year.

Clearly, these allegations provoke the passion of all but the most hardened of skeptics, and, invariably, this passionate response hinders objectivity and a search for evidence to substantiate these allegations. The conspiracy proponents have successfully dragged the issue of Satanism into an emotional quagmire of outrage and disbelief.

In an attempt to warn the public of the influence of Satanism, others have taken a single case study and generalized its findings, causing even greater confusion. Some of the most widely read works in this literature of Satanism are simply the gross generalizations of one individual who is attempting to exploit a bizarre experience. This is an effective marketing strategy, good for sales, but ineffective in furthering our understanding of the subject.

One example, the national organization "Bothered About Dungeons and Dragons", or BADD for short, was founded by a well-intended anti-Satan crusader from Virginia by the name of Patricia Pulling (1989; Stackpole, 1989). Pulling maintains that fantasy role-playing games like

Dungeons and Dragons are responsible for the recent proliferation of young people involved in Satanism. She became involved in this campaign after the tragic suicide of her son, who was apparently obsessed with Dungeons and Dragons.

Such extrapolation of a single case is not unique to Pulling's organization. The Parents' Music Resource Center (1986), known as PMRC, argues that Satanism, among other maladies, can be the result of musical lyrics that glamorize serious emotional problems of the adolescent. Their position is based on arguments drawn from the literature on subliminal perception, much of which is no longer accepted as useful. Essentially, the argument is that the listener will acquire messages that are conveyed below the level of detection but influence one's values and attitudes.

Some advocates of Satanism suffer from a similar problem by supporting a philosophy based solely on their personal experiences. Anton LaVey, for example, perhaps the best known Satanist in this country, makes assumptions about the world of Satanism from the narrow scope of his personal experience in the circus world. His authority as a philosopher is steeped in the circus world of showmanship and illusion, estranged from the experiences of mainstream society.

LaVey sees the human species as an emotionally primitive group that holds vengeance and carnal pleasures as its highest priority. His major work, *The Satanic Bible,* has had an enormous impact on the lives of many adolescents who have found its arguments sympathetic to their emotional troubles. This book, and its influence on young people, is discussed in detail in a later chapter.

THIS WRITER'S ASSUMPTIONS

This book is written with some assumptions that should be made clear to the reader in advance. First, I believe that Satanism contributes to a propagation of evil in the world and is, therefore, objectionable. It is especially insidious to young people who have not yet objectively formulated a philosophy of life in a context apart from their adolescent emotional problems.

Second, I believe objectivity is essential to our ability to help another person effectively. For many people, the idea of devil worship provokes strong emotion. Helping a young person understand the problem of Satanism cannot be done when we are reacting emotionally. Our anger, fear, and frustration come from a lack of understanding. From ignorance and misinformation come inaccurate and impulsive solutions. Neither works. We can only begin to help young people if we approach the problem with an objective understanding of Satanism. The focus of this book is to provide that understanding. Much of the misinformation proposed by self-proclaimed experts about Satanism hinders an effective understanding of the problem. There are too many single-issue people who propose solutions based on a narrow point of view. To be effective, we must view the problem of Satanism from a perspective that considers what we know about human development and the ways in which individuals develop problems of psychopathology.

Third, the problem is not Satanism itself. Satanism is the symptom. Those who fail to recognize the causal relationship between problem and symptom will also fail to understand that most of the outrageous activity associated with Satanism is simply evidence that something has gone seriously awry in the life of the young person behaving this way. We cannot hope to solve the problem simply by attempting to eliminate the symptom. This only results in making the serious Satanist more careful and the potential Satanist more curious.

Fourth, I believe that religious experience is helpful to the development of a young person. Religious training, however, when given to a child in a heavy-handed manner that exploits fear, can have dangerous consequences. We have an obligation to perceptively observe and monitor the effect of religion on our children.

Fifth, there are major differences between religious cults and Satanic cults. This book is intended only to provide an understanding of why and how young people are attracted to Satanic cults. There are some excellent books that explain the issues of religious cults. The reader interested in that problem is referred to Galanter's *Cults: Faith Healing and Coercion* (1989), MacHovec's *Cults and Personality* (1989) and Conway and Siegleman's *Snapping: America's Sudden Epidemic of Personality Change* (1979). These works do not, however, address the dynamics of Satanic cult involvement. Satanism and religious cults are different concerns and must be considered separately.

Finally, this book is written with a full awareness of an individual's rights to do what he or she pleases, as long as it does not injure another or interfere with another's rights. Consequently, this book does not take the position that any occult belief system can or should be abolished. Satanism, however, is objectionable for children and adolescents on psychological grounds. The beliefs themselves, as we will see, are not the primary issue. The fact that adolescents have come to exploit the implications of these beliefs is really the problem.

Parents, educators, clergy, and mental health professionals have a personal and professional obligation to obtain an objective view of Satanism. One day we may have the responsibility to sit face to face with a young person who is curious about, enamored with, or involved in Satanism. Depending on our response, that first encounter will either reduce or advance his or her interest. To engage in such a significant encounter without psychologically sound and objective information is futile.

DISCLAIMERS

Satanism is a belief system and philosophy of life that mocks the values and practices of the traditionally accepted mainstream religions of the Judeo-Christian tradition. As such, it is a problem that impacts the individual's psychological development, religious training, personal experience, and the culture in which the person lives.

This book does not address evil in general as a problem in the world. It does not address other occult practices, psychiatric problems, or religious cults. It focuses exclusively on problems associated with the individual who finds Satanism to be a viable option during adolescent development. The following groups are specifically not a focus of this book.

WITCHCRAFT

There are many people in this country who practice witchcraft. Of these, there are two basic types, white witches and black witches. The former engage themselves in the practice of worshipping gods and goddesses of nature: wind, earth, planets, fire, and other forces of nature. They typically enjoin these forces to obtain good of some sort. They have nothing to do with the practice of Satanism and should not be confused with Satanism. Readers interested in this area of occult practice will find Cunningham's *The Truth about Witchcraft Today* (1988) appropriate.

Black witches may be considered a part of the evil in the world. They implore the forces of nature to inflict punishment on other people, using spells and other bizarre incantations. While black witches may be involved in the proliferation of evil in the world, they are not Satanists. This book does not address the problems of black witchcraft. Hill and

Williams, in *The Supernatural* (1965), provide an objective history of this area of witchcraft and its role in contemporary society.

SANTERIA

There are large numbers of people who practice Santeria, a combination of Catholicism, the worship of the spirits of dead people, and the religious beliefs of the victims of the slave trade, principally from Nigeria. These people worship their dead ancestors, who are believed to inhabit the spirit world, not unlike Catholics praying to the saints for favors. Although Santeria does not promote evil, it can involve the practice of animal sacrifice, leading some people to believe that Santeria is related to the general practice of Satanism. It is in no way related. This book does not address Santeria or any of the problems that some people might believe are associated with it. The California Office of Criminal Justice Planning (1990) has published a monograph that provides an excellent overview of the elements of Santeria and other relatively obscure occult practices, including the Carribean Palo Mayombe and Mexican Brujeria.

VOODOO

When African slaves were transported to the Western Hemisphere, they were "converted" to Christianity. This process of alleged conversion was predicated on the assumption that these slaves had a "pagan" religion that should be replaced by Christianity. These people, especially in areas outside of the United States, held on to many of their early African traditions. What resulted from these attempts to convert them was a hybridization of early African religious tradition and Christianity that came to be known as voodoo. The practitioners of voodoo and their priests, the vodouns, are not Satanists. While their religious practices and rituals are quite unusual, and fascinating from an anthropological perspective, they do not engage in any form of devil worship associated with Satanism. Davis (1985) has written an excellent book, *The Serpent and the Rainbow,* that describes voodoo and its powerful impact on contemporary Haitian culture.

MULTIPLE PERSONALITY DISORDERS

There are a number of psychiatric patients, many of whom are not hospitalized, who suffer from any one of a variety of problems that involve the development of multiple personalities. These people have suffered serious trauma in their lives and have developed different personalities to cope with these problems. They are often the victims of severe physical and sexual abuse. These people are in need of information and help to understand what has happened to them. On some occasions, one personality may take the form of the devil or some other evil persona. That desperate coping attempt does not make the individual a Satanist. It simply says there is serious psychopathology affecting the personality. This book will not provide them with the answers they need. These individuals need the advice of a professional who can either help them or direct them to an appropriate referral. Most professional literature on the subject of psychopathology includes a consideration of this problem. Crabtree (1985) has written a helpful book on multiple personality disorders intended for a lay audience, *Multiple Man: Explorations in Possession and Multiple Personality.*

MULTIGENERATIONAL CULT FAMILIES

Some people are involved in Satanism because they have been born into a family that has practiced Satanism for many years, perhaps through several generations. Hence the name multigenerational cults. Individuals introduced to Satanism in this manner are entirely different from the adolescent who finds Satanism a convenient means of expression of adolescent anger and frustration. This book will not address the problems experienced by members of multigenerational cult families. Since so little is known about these groups, there is no objective resource available to assist an interested reader in obtaining further information.

THE FOCUS OF THIS BOOK

This book will address several areas. In Chapter 2 we will describe the different personality types that are drawn to Satanism for solutions of adolescent problems. In Chapter 3 we will explore the factors that determine whether a young person is at risk of becoming involved in

Satanic cults. Chapter 4 provides an explanation of the basic principles espoused by Anton LaVey in *The Satanic Bible*. The next three chapters are devoted to the psychological significance of power, the impact of dualities, and the role of ritual in the phenomenon of Satanic involvement.

Chapter 8 will address issues of parenting that have a bearing on a young person's vulnerability for involvement. Chapter 9 addresses communication in three areas: general barriers to effective communication, the ways in which communication is facilitated in crisis situations, and, finally, some suggestions for communicating with an adolescent who is already involved in Satanism.

In Chapter 10 we will look at the relationship between Satanism and the problem of adolescent suicide, concluding that this combination can be deadly for a young person. Finally, Chapter 11 reviews ten general conclusions that parents and others working with young people need to keep in mind.

2

Personality Types of Adolescents Involved in Satanism

The emotional and behavioral problems of adolescents who practice Satanism and its rituals are of increasing concern to parents, teachers, and mental health professionals (Moriarty & Story, 1990). Satanists generally hold that Satan represents the antithesis of Jesus Christ, and they stand for values opposite to those held by Christianity (LaVey, 1969). Many of these adolescents are dabblers, young people who undertake an interest in Satanism without seriously evaluating the implications of that pursuit (Simandl & Naysmith, 1988).

There is need for a better understanding of the impact of Satanism on the emotional problems of adolescents who follow its beliefs and practice its rituals. Satanism is not a unitary problem for which a single prescription for treatment can routinely be ordered. Many efforts to describe the process of adolescent involvement in Satanism fail to discern the different reasons why adolescents find Satanism attractive. They generally assume the problem to be generic in nature, implying that both a single cause and treatment strategy is indicated (Wheeler, Wood, & Hatch, 1988). Other articles, in the literature of law enforcement, address only the signs and symptoms of involvement (Holmes, 1989; Lanning, 1989). They assume that solutions to the problem are found in approaches characterized by symptom reduction or symptom suppression.

This chapter will describe four personality types of young people who find themselves drawn to Satanism. While the pattern of adopting Satanism has similar characteristics for all adolescents, different kinds of symptoms emerge that are related to different personality types. As these differences are discerned by the parent, teacher, or counselor, a more appropriate choice of intervention will enhance the effectiveness of any attempt to help. While the pattern of adopting Satanism is similar for most adolescents, its implications are significantly affected by the individual's personality, the beginnings of which can be traced to early life experiences.

In the same way that adolescents suffer emotional problems for different reasons, they are also attracted to Satanic cult involvement for different reasons. This chapter will be of assistance to parents, teachers, clergy, and counselors as they struggle to evaluate the effect of Satanism on the personality and behavior of the young person.

PSYCHOLOGICAL IMPLICATIONS OF SATANISM

The implications of adolescent Satanism create a host of psychological issues for those attempting to help young people. While some counselors report they are seeing more adolescents in therapy who have some cult involvement (Bourget, Gagnon, & Bradford, 1988; Moriarty & Story, 1990; Wheeler, Wood, & Hatch, 1988), they also report that little assistance is available for evaluating the effect of cult involvement on underlying emotional problems. Determining the degree of emotional impact of Satanic cult involvement is the first task of the mental health professional. More specifically, the question is "What types of problems motivate this cult involvement, and what are their causes?" A closer scrutiny of the motives and personality types of adolescents drawn to Satanic cults will provide useful clues.

It has been my experience as a clinical psychologist that the majority of those youngsters who become involved in Satanism are, indeed, dabblers (Simandl & Naysmith, 1989), adolescents who are at an early stage of cult involvement. They bring to the Satanic cult experience any number of significant preexisting emotional problems. These young people find Satanism to be an effective vehicle by which they can vent the anger and frustration caused by these underlying emotional problems. The process of accepting Satanism is a simple but powerful solution to a variety of emotional problems.

Satanism has appeal to different adolescents for different reasons. In an earlier article (Moriarty & Story, 1990), two general factors were related to Satanism: parent relationships and the developmental tasks of adolescence. Just as we see different personalities develop in adolescence, these differences play themselves out in different styles of relating to parents and in the ways that major developmental tasks of adolescence are addressed. From this point of view, four types of Satanic dabblers emerge, and each requires a different strategy for intervention to be effective.

A DIFFERENTIAL PERSPECTIVE

Some treatment strategies operate on the assumption that Satanic involvement is symptomatic of a major psychiatric disorder and view Satanism from a more general problem known as a Multiple Personality Disorder (American Psychiatric Association, 1987). This diagnosis is commonly characteristic of victims of multigenerational cults, a relatively rare phenomenon, the scope of which is beyond the intent of this book.

A narrow view of the Satanic dabbler, however, may tempt a helpful individual to intervene with a single strategy in every case of adolescent involvement. The popular literature would indicate that this strategy for intervention should be symptom reduction or symptom suppression (e.g., Anderson, 1988).

The following represents a general model of different types that attempts to provide a better understanding of the basic differences between Satanic cult members. The model is based on experience, intuition, and some speculation about adolescents and Satanic cults. As our understanding of this phenomenon grows, we may find additions and alterations to this strategy for differential diagnosis, but this model has proven useful in the planning of intervention strategies for adolescent Satanists in the dabbler stage. The four types of dabblers are Psychopathic Delinquents, Angry Misfits, Pseudo-Intellectuals, and Suicidal Impulsives. Each of these types is qualitatively different from the others and requires that different intervention strategies be considered before a counselor attempts a diagnosis or intervention plan. There may also be others as yet unidentified.

THE PSYCHOPATHIC DELINQUENT

CHARACTERISTICS: Cruel, demeaning, aggressive, violent
MOTIVATION: Satanism justifies criminal action

EMOTIONAL BENEFIT: The domination of others
DSM III-R CORRELATE: Sadistic Personality Disorder
INTERVENTION STRATEGY: Prosecution

> A sixteen-year-old male is referred for counseling by the court. He has a long history of drug abuse, violent acts toward people and animals, and sexual acting out. He has been a victim of abuse as a young child and feels emotionally close to no one. His problems of failing at school are complicated by chronic truancy and behavioral problems. His initial involvement in criminal activity began at the age of ten when he was arrested for theft.

This type of adolescent finds the violence of Satanic ritual and the degradation of others to be extremely attractive. He (this type is almost always a male) cares little and understands less about Satanic belief systems and has no concern for reasons why Satanism is practiced. His involvement with paraphernalia used for rituals is most likely to involve the possession of knives rather than candles, books, robes, or other items. He is most likely a heavy drug user and is probably involved in a variety of criminal activities in the community as well.

Law enforcement personnel report a close connection between Satanism and the availability of drugs. Some Satanists are alleged to use the lure of drugs to recruit members (Lyons, 1988). The combined fascination with violence, bloodletting, and sexual abuse of women makes the Psychopathic Delinquent extremely difficult to treat and potentially dangerous to the community if left to his own devices.

The primary focus on Satanic dabblers exhibiting this pattern of pathology should be the criminality of their behavior and the subsequent need for incarceration concurrent with any attempt at intervention. Their behavior patterns are descriptive of an undersocialized aggressive type of delinquent described by Quay (1987) and a sadistic personality disorder (301.90 NOS) identified in DSM III-R (American Psychiatric Association, 1987). These individuals are highly resistant to treatment and, according to Quay, have "the most pessimistic prognosis for adult adjustment" (1987, p. 122).

There is little doubt that this type of individual will bring to the therapist a long history of serious emotional disturbance. It is a potentially serious treatment error for anyone to conclude that Satanism caused this pattern of hostile and violent behavior. On the contrary, the sadistic personality is attracted to Satanism as an opportunity to acquire power and domination in an arena where such expression is sanctioned and even necessary to the pursuit of the cult belief system. Since this sadistic nature of violence is rewarded rather than punished, this type of dabbler may pose a significant risk to the physical well-being of others. This individual presents an extremely difficult set of problems that makes counseling unlikely to succeed and hospitalization an equally frustrating intervention, as well. Therapeutic intervention requires a close monitoring of the individual's compliance. Millon (1981) suggests that supervised self-help groups that allow a free discussion of attitudes may be useful in dealing with this problem. Prosecution is the only effective first step in any attempt to intervene with this type of adolescent Satanist. A prerequisite to any treatment is a closely structured environment that guarantees no access to drugs, sadistic activity, or the trappings of Satanic rituals.

 **THE ANGRY MISFIT**

CHARACTERISTICS:	Sulky, irritable, argumentative, critical of others
MOTIVATION:	Satanism is a vehicle for social acceptance
EMOTIONAL BENEFIT:	Affiliation and group support
DSM III-R CORRELATE:	Oppositional disorder
INTERVENTION STRATEGY:	Redirection of anger

A fourteen-year-old female is referred for therapy. She has a history of indiscriminate expression of anger in school. She is vehement in her blaming of others for her miserable condition. She cannot maintain a relationship with neighborhood boys despite exaggerated attempts to do so. Temporary relationships always end in an explosive outburst of anger and frustration that put her at some risk of serious violence. She finds a circle of older friends who are not known to her family or to school personnel. She clings tenaciously to these friendships while cloaking them in a veil of secrecy.

The second dabbler type, the Angry Misfit, follows the lead of the psychopathic delinquent. This adolescent brings to Satanic involvement a long history of impulsive behavior and repressed anger. As a child, this individual's behavior was symptomatic of an oppositional defiant disorder (DSM III-R: 313.81), including a good deal of acting out that stops short of the overt hostility observed in the behavior of the psychopathic delinquent. The distinguishing features between the Angry Misfit and the Psychopathic Delinquent are two.

First, the Psychopathic Delinquent is comfortable escalating his or her behavior to levels of violence and sadistic acts. The Angry Misfit obtains vicarious satisfaction from observing this activity but is not a direct participant in it. Secondly, the Psychopathic Delinquent invests little energy in attempting to justify his or her behavior while the Angry Misfit finds it extremely important to hold someone or something responsible for his or her actions. Without some object on which to place blame for his or her action, the Angry Misfit loses the ability to act with a comfortable level of perceived justification. It is common to see the Angry Misfit going to great lengths to justify his or her behavior. The absence of logic in this process of blame is evidence that the angry misfit is in great distress.

Because the style of coping is typically irritable and argumentative, the Angry Misfit often has many experiences of being rejected by others, making appropriate peer group relationships inordinately difficult to sustain over any length of time. As a result, a dual attraction to Satanic cult activity results.

First, it provides an organized system to facilitate the placing of blame on the outside world for the Angry Misfit's problems. Second, the Angry Misfit is accepted by other Satanists, thereby providing a sense of belonging that fulfills a basic and pressing need. These factors create powerful bonds and dependency relationships that have little to do with cult philosophy or belief systems. To be successful, a plan to help must address these dependency needs. Second, intervention must facilitate the appropriate expression of anger when experienced by this type of young Satanist.

Since the Angry Misfit is vigilant to opportunities to justify anger, an approach that carefully broaches emotional issues is recommended. A cognitive therapy approach that lends objectivity to the Angry Misfit's emotional issues will allow the therapist to avoid provoking outbursts of anger and subsequent attempts to justify it. The likelihood that the dependency needs will be transferred to the therapist is also significant. It is, therefore, important that the counselor take good care in addressing termination issues with the Angry Misfit. Finally, these clients will try the patience of a therapist and are likely to encourage early termination.

Counselors or parents may find that this type of adolescent Satanist spends a good deal of time listening to heavy metal music. Although many people think that heavy metal music leads to Satanism, a causal relationship between music and Satanism has not been established. However, since the rhythm and beat of this music commonly stimulates the vicarious expression of hostility and aggression, it appears that a musical preoccupation by the Angry Misfit may be a subconscious attempt at self-cure for someone who is already involved with Satanism. If the cult or its members are not available to lend justification to the Angry Misfit at times when his or her anger is escalating, developing a dependency on heavy metal music may provide for some venting of anger when this Satanist is separated from fellow cult members. My conjecture is that some heavy metal music allows the adolescent to sublimate anger and frustration, making it more manageable, and the attachment to a Satanic cult may be greatly encouraged by an intense need to unload pent-up anger.

THE PSEUDO-INTELLECTUAL

CHARACTERISTICS:	Grandiose sense of self-importance preoccupied with fantasies of power
MOTIVATION:	Satanism provides superior knowledge
EMOTIONAL BENEFIT:	The illusion of intellectual superiority
DSM III-R CORRELATE:	Narcissistic personality disorder
INTERVENTION STRATEGY:	Reassessment of personal belief systems

> A seventeen-year-old male is referred for counseling by his mother. He was in a gifted school program until the tenth grade, whereupon he lost interest in school, claiming it was too boring. He continues to be a voracious reader and recently has taken a keen interest in the occult. He has several friends who are enamored with his knowledge and follow him around. His mother reports that she knows very little about where he spends his time.

The third type of dabbler, the Pseudo-Intellectual, derives his or her satisfaction from the pursuit of ideas. The perception of power attained by knowledge of the occult is a major reinforcer. He or she is likely to be much less hostile or aggressive than his or her previously described dabbler types. Any aggressive needs observed in the Pseudo-Intellectual are channeled into the formation of ideas and a philosophical development that represents personal power and the domination of others through intellectual means. The illusion of intellectual superiority also provides this dabbler with the belief that knowledge of the occult is necessary and sufficient to resist therapeutic intervention. He or she is likely to be diagnosed as having a narcissistic personality disorder (301.81), according to DSM III-R diagnostic criteria (American Psychiatric Association, 1987). Engaging this adolescent in a discussion of the merits of Satanism is likely to result in the individual being further encouraged to adopt this belief system since he or she has developed great facility in the defense of these beliefs.

Basic to the dynamics of the Pseudo-Intellectual is a need to gain superiority over the other cult members by acquiring and flaunting a superior knowledge of the occult. As a result, this type of individual is likely to be far more knowledgeable about matters of Satanism than any concerned adult who attempts to intervene.

This knowledge base provides the foundation for a general attitude of grandiosity. These dabblers feel inordinate power and self-importance from having a position of expertise among other cult members. Consequently, an attempt to intervene with this individual by discussing the relative merits of Satanism, for example, is not likely to be a useful strategy. The knowledge obtained by the Pseudo-Intellectual is less significant than the means by which that information has been accepted as valid.

For example, in any discussion with a Pseudo-Intellectual, a parent or counselor is likely to see evidence of a weakness in critical thinking skills. It is likely that this type of adolescent cult dabbler commonly engages in the process of deciding upon what is true in a belief system in an imprecise and careless manner. As a result, an intervention addressing the process of belief, that is, how we decide to believe that something is true, is more effective and potentially more useful than a strategy that attempts to confront the beliefs themselves. While claiming to be very intellectual, they usually report beliefs predicated on the basis of information that is seriously lacking in logic or substance. In many cases, these Satanists believe that truth is that which is found in the printed word. Having read a book (of their choice) makes it unequivocally true.

These adolescents need to be engaged in constructive dialogue to allow them to recognize that their adoption of beliefs is more a matter of internal frustrations than it is the result of a critical thinking process. Individuals attempting to help this adolescent should be aware of the importance of engaging the adolescent in a dialogue that is not perceived as threatening and nurtures a relationship that encourages self-exploration.

Consequently, what the adolescent knows is far less important than how he or she has come to accept this knowledge as reality. An intervention found helpful is to address the question, "How do you know what you know?" in a variety of ways. Focusing discussion on any one of the common beliefs held by the Pseudo-Intellectual may be an effective forum for this discussion.

THE SUICIDAL IMPULSIVE

CHARACTERISTICS:	Self-destructiveness, lack of concern for personal safety
MOTIVATION:	Satanism gives a rationalization for suicidal thinking
EMOTIONAL BENEFIT:	Holding life on the edge of death
DSM III-R CORRELATE:	Antisocial personality disorder
INTERVENTION STRATEGY:	Hospitalization: Suicidal assessment

A fifteen-year-old male is referred for counseling. He has a history of self-destructive behavior; two of these incidents have been serious attempts at suicide. His mother assures the counselor that he will "grow out of it" and this is "just a phase." He has recently been carving designs in his arms that mean "nothing" to him.

The fourth dabbler type, the Suicidal Impulsive, may be the most clinically disturbed of the four types identified in this discussion. This adolescent approaches Satanic cult involvement with reckless abandon, impressing others with his or her great propensity for risk taking. He or she is likely to fall within the diagnostic criteria of the DSM III-R antisocial personality disorder (301.70, American Psychiatric Association, 1987). The necessary prerequisite for this type of Satanic cult involvement is a serious lack of concern for one's safety and personal well-being. Beneath this show of daring is a serious problem of suicidal ideation.

The combination of Satanic involvement and suicidal ideation presents a significant challenge to any parent or counselor. Many times this young man or woman cannot be given the necessary help without being hospitalized. In all cases, the degree of Satanic involvement should be given careful consideration in developing a strategy for reintegrating this adolescent back to his or her environment.

The adolescent of this personality type is likely to have an intense feeling of lacking control of his or her environment. He or she concedes to the struggle for control by toying with control over his or her own life. As a result, there is a significant motivation to put his or her life on the edge of existence as an exercise of control. There is a particularly significant problem in the area of suicide potential because this adolescent begins to connect the Satanic cult to the suicidal rituals believed to be a test of an individual's commitment to Satan. Johnston (1989) and Lyons (1988) discuss cases of individuals who have determined that the act of suicide is a worthy act of homage to Satan.

A double bind results from the clash of preexisting suicidal ideation and the acceptance of suicide as a part of the cult philosophy and associated ritual. The potential for this justification of suicide is a significant factor in the motivation of the Suicidal Impulsive to become involved in Satanic dabbling.

If fear or guilt have kept this adolescent from acting on suicidal ideation in the past, it is possible that the ritualization and mysticism of Satanic cult rituals involving suicidal pacts with Satan will provide sufficient external and authoritative justification for an adolescent to act on these suicidal thoughts.

In trying to help this troubled young person, the assessment of suicidal risk is the most important and obvious factor. Ordinarily, the risk of suicide declines with the passage of time from the previous crisis or attempt (Shneidman, 1985). However, in cases of adolescents involved in Satanic cults, the opposite is likely to be true. The adolescent who makes a suicidal gesture or a significant attempt may be separated for a period of time from his or her cult connections either through hospitalization or through the careful monitoring of associations. During this time of separation, the risk for a repeat attempt is diminished considerably. However, with attempts to reintegrate the adolescent back to his or her environment, the connections between the adolescent and Satanic cult relationships are readily reestablished. Therefore, the risk for a repeat attempt may increase over time and be the opposite of what is expected in other cases of suicidal thought.

A plan for intervention should give careful consideration to removing this adolescent from his or her immediate social environment to provide extensive therapeutic intervention that effectively ensures the individual's safety and welfare. Finally, many troubled adolescents, especially when suicide is a factor, are likely to be experiencing more than one serious disorder. As a result, they should be evaluated for a dual diagnosis, that is, the likelihood of two major problems affecting their lives. A significant number of these adolescents, for example, will also be experiencing drug and alcohol problems, which must also be addressed in an effective plan of intervention.

CONCLUSION

From a diagnostic viewpoint, the impact of Satanism is best understood as a presenting problem, that is, one that serves to mask underlying emotional problems that are not readily apparent. The problems also long predate Satanic involvement. These personality problems may be represented by any one of the four types described in this chapter. Counselors and others need to proceed carefully with adolescents who demonstrate Satanic involvement and to look beyond the common symptom pattern and focus treatment efforts on these underlying problems. The fact that different personalities share common symptoms of Satanic practice should not dissuade us from searching out the different patterns of motivation that underlie common signs of Satanic cult involvement. Effective intervention requires that these differences be identified and given primary consideration in a treatment plan.

As parents, teachers, and counselors become more involved with adolescents dabbling in Satanism, other personality types may be identified. Despite much of the hoopla that has recently been made of adolescent Satanism, it must be viewed as a mental health problem symptomatic of preexisting emotional problems. All of us dedicated to this effort need to be alert to underlying personality disorders in the intervention process and treatment planning.

3

Risk Factors Associated
with Satanism

When young people become involved in Satanism, often their parents are unaware until there are serious consequences that demand intervention. Because many young people can be redirected from this involvement if it is recognized early, parents should be alert to patterns that may indicate vulnerability to cults in the lives of their children. Cultural, physical, psychological, and social factors must be considered when assessing a young person's susceptibility to or involvement in Satanism.

CULTURAL FACTORS

In our attempts to evaluate the personal vulnerability of young people to the influence of Satanism, there are six cultural factors that should be considered during risk assessment: (1) the complexity of society, (2) the loss of psychological anchors, (3) the absence of role models, (4) emotionally unavailable parents, (5) academic demands, and (6) peer pressure.

Greater Complexity

People working with adolescents need to be sensitive to the fact that growing up during the end of this century is far more difficult for young people than it was at any previous time in history. Young people today are exposed to many temptations and concerns that were not a significant part of their elders' adolescent lives. The drug epidemic, for example, has taken an enormous toll on the youth of America. In addition, street gangs are infiltrating communities far beyond the boundaries of the inner city. The reality of AIDS (Acquired Immune Deficiency Syndrome) has invaded the personal arena of adolescent sexuality, inalterably shaking the core of personal security for many people.

Given these complications, young people may find it increasingly more difficult to maintain the values and attitudes we might like them to hold. It is important for parents to convey a sensitive understanding of the complexity of these demands while continuing to hold high expectations for their behavior.

Decline of Family Anchors

Some sociologists argue that many of society's problems are the result of change occurring at too rapid a rate. This argument holds when you consider how many of society's traditional religious and family anchors have been lost in the last few decades.

Our culture is becoming increasingly more transient, with families in America moving once every three to five years. Goldsmith and Clark (1987) report that 8 million school-age children move to new schools and new communities each year. This transience causes an ongoing problem of adjustment for many young people. Lack of rootedness is typically a source of considerable anxiety. Parents who move frequently need to realize that their children often have more difficulty adjusting to these moves than they are likely to express.

Lack of Adult Role Models

Many young people today are growing up on their own. The number of children from single-parent families and from families in which both parents work is dramatic. As a result, young people are often left without sufficient exposure to their parents as role models. They cope by constructing images of adulthood either from fantasies or from what television or rock stars offer as models. Personal time perspective is increasingly distorted by television, and many children are being led to believe that problems must be solved in sixty minutes. They have been deprived of experiencing the curative power of the passage of time in dealing with emotional problems.

The compression of time in the lives of young people erodes their regard for the passage of time as a healing element. As a result, many young people find themselves responding impulsively to problems, not having been shown the lessons of a patient and sensitive adult. As a result, they fail to acquire a sense of meaningful future time and how it can be a curative factor in their lives.

Emotional Unavailability of Parents

Many young people live in families where parents are so involved with their own complicated lives that the children are left to deal with their own problems alone. The busy, successful, and detached parent who is unavailable emotionally to the child in times of trouble is an all-too-common theme. When children find themselves in emotional turmoil, they typically look first to their parents for help. When their parents are unavailable, they look elsewhere. In our society there are many people willing to present themselves as friends to our children when, in fact, their motives have little to do with the welfare of the child. These emotionally needy adolescents are attracted to that which their parents have failed to provide.

Academic Demands

The fifth cultural factor relates to the intense academic pressure and complexity that many children experience in junior high school and high school. The common expressions of concern over the decline of academic achievement in this country overshadow the efforts that many young people put into their responsibilities. When we fail to respond sensitively to these efforts, we create frustrations that are not likely to be revealed to us until later. These young people often will look outside the home for greater consolation and empathy. Satanism is an effective means to meeting these needs.

Futurists tell us that the amount of knowledge in the world doubles approximately every three years. As a result, some young people find that pursuing academic excellence is an exercise in futility, their preparation for a future career rendered useless by the rate and pace of change observed in many fields. Because of their resulting frustrations, they are likely to invest their energies elsewhere, dismissing the future with a global denial of its significance and meaning to the present.

Peer Pressure

Children and teenagers can create terrible peer pressure conflicts for each other. Most children have the common ability to be extremely cruel and inflexible in their evaluations of each other. They also have the capacity to forgive more quickly than their parents. This creates a serious problem if young people are making decisions after they experience this cruelty and rejection, but before they experience the forgiveness that often follows.

The issue of timing for young people dealing with peer group pressure is important for two reasons. First, a major source of stress in our lives comes from the frustrations that are encountered in handling interpersonal relationships. Second, one of the major roadblocks to the management of conflicts with children is the relative inability of some parents to forgive their children when they behave badly. Many parents continue to be angry about something their child has done long after the child has recovered and, in many cases, forgotten what the conflict was about in the first place. While children and adolescents can be more flexible in dealing with conflicts, they can also be much more impulsive.

PHYSICAL FACTORS

Four factors related to the physical development of a child are significant to our evaluation of risk. When these factors are out of the range of normal development, something is usually wrong and should be addressed by the appropriate professional. The areas of concern to us are changes in body weight, sleep disturbance, clothing styles, and frequent illnesses.

Body Weight

Children and adolescents are creatures of habit. As a result, they behave predictably, especially in areas that involve their established routines. For example, a noticeable change in body weight out of proportion to the normal growth and development is an indicator of a problem. Weight gain or loss may be associated with certain drug use, it may be associated with dealing with anxiety in an ineffective manner, or it may be due to the onset of a physical problem. In any of these cases, something is not going properly in the life of the young person and should not be ignored.

Sleep Habits

Children and adolescents are normally good sleepers. Any change in the sleep habits of a young person is likely the result of psychological or physical stress. If stress levels interfere with the routine of a child to the extent that sleep is disturbed, it suggests the influence of emotional turmoil that is not being appropriately dealt with during the waking hours. In the symbolic context of one's emotional life, sleep represents a loss of control and a lowering of psychological defenses. As a result, emotional conflicts and stressors tend to creep out and the unconscious conflicts that surface during sleep can seriously disrupt sleep patterns.

Clothing Styles

Some parents report that a child in early adolescence will suddenly adopt a radically different style of dress. This is commonly associated with fads that hold power over early teens and is a function of the impact of advertising on young people. It may also be indicative of a young person's expressing a need to belong to a peer group or to emulate a subculture that is represented through popular music. Wearing a concert T-shirt, for example, can be a major status symbol for some young people.

In some cases, however, it is also associated with the adoption of Satanic cult ideas. Many young people who become involved in such cults will subtly reveal their involvement through a change in their dress and clothing. Symbols ornamenting clothing and jewelry are obvious and easily recognizable. Most common are the pentagram, a five-pointed encircled star, or an inverted cross. In some cases teens are simply adopting the trappings of certain heavy metal music groups, but in other cases such adornment may signify that an adolescent is becoming enamored with Satanic activity.

Frequent Illnesses

Finally, one of the warning signs of youngsters involved in problems related to Satanism is a pattern of suspicious illnesses that result in absence from school. This is especially significant when a youngster reports or claims to be ill during the week but suddenly recovers for the weekend. When this pattern begins to be established, it has two implications that are significant. First, the use of drugs in certain cult activity may cause legitimate illness, especially bronchitis or respiratory problems. Second, in families where both parents work, this claim of illness provides a young person with the opportunity to have an entire day free without parental supervision. A major requisite for cult involvement is secrecy, and young people who cannot find a feeling of personal power in the real world will find it in a world of covert activities.

PSYCHOLOGICAL FACTORS

The individual attraction to Satanism does not occur in a vacuum. Both preceding and concurrent with the signs and symptoms of Satanic involvement are a number of changes in the emotional life of the young person. Parents, counselors, and others concerned with promoting the mental health of young people need to be alert to these changes because they are precursors to a pattern of involvement that can have serious consequences in the life of a young person. Eleven areas are of greatest concern: (1) perceptual threat levels, (2) rigid thinking, (3) impulsivity, (4) motivation changes, (5) stress levels, (6) changes in self-concept, (7) spontaneous remission, (8) anger management, (9) guilt, (10) the reversal of feelings, and (11) bonding changes.

Perceptual Threat

First, an adolescent at risk may show signs of perceptual threat. The emotional tension brought on by perceptual threat restricts an individual's ability to view alternatives and choices, rendering the young person incapable of dealing effectively with problems. Events that cause perceptual threat interfere with judgment and decision-making ability. As a result, poor judgment and an increased level of tension is commonly associated with children and adolescents who are becoming exposed to greater risk. The most common indication of perceptual threat is the onset of intolerant and impulsive behavior that appears, on the surface, to indicate irrational or unintelligent behavior.

Rigid Thinking Patterns

Second, thinking patterns become more rigid. One of the hallmarks of good mental health is the ability to be tolerant of various points of view. Often when young people become involved in Satanism they create thinking patterns that become dichotomous, patterns that see only the extremes of a situation. The adolescent becomes very defensive of ideas that he or she agrees with and responds negatively to ideas with which he or she does not agree. The major consequence of rigid thinking is that it impairs the adolescent's ability to critically evaluate a belief system. It becomes totally rejected or totally embraced.

This can result in a "we versus them" mentality that causes young people to blindly defend their friends and become increasingly dependent on them. As a result, they sacrifice their sense of identity to a group and fail in the essential task of developing their own personal individuality.

Greater Impulsiveness

The third area of risk assessment involves increased impulsiveness. In many cases young people experiencing emotional turmoil have lost their ability to handle frustration and conflict. They tend to fly off the handle more frequently than their friends. These impulsive displays of anger are a clear indication that something is raising the frustration level of the child or adolescent. More importantly, it is an indication that the adolescent is struggling to ignore sources of anger by pretending they do not exist. Repressed anger and how it is displaced are common symptoms of the behavior of young people who are drawn to the Satanism for solutions to their problems.

Lack of Motivation

The fourth area of assessment involves what was once called the "amotivational syndrome." Historically, the amotivational syndrome was a term used to describe the chronic drug user whose seeming lack of motivation was actually a redirected pattern of motivation. What was really going on was that the drug users were so highly motivated to pursue drugs that they appeared to have little motivation to do anything else. *Amotivational* was an incorrect term, since it implied a lack of motivation to do anything, when these individuals were in fact highly motivated to obtain drugs.

When young people are involved in the beginning stages of emotional problems they often lose interest in the activities that previously held their interest. A superficial assessment of their patterns of interest and motivation might appear to be "amotivational." What is really happening is the refocusing and rechanneling of emotional energy in coping with the problem. Coping is done in a way that proves unsettling to parents who, themselves, deny what is going on. Even more often there is a pursuit of ideas, beliefs, and practices that must be held in secrecy, as stealth is an essential ingredient in the practice of Satanism.

General Stress Management

The fifth area of assessment involves general stress levels. Young people normally tend to be somewhat impulsive and act out there emotions more readily than adults. However, these routine periods of emotional expression are usually followed by a rapid recovery; they express themselves intensely, recover from whatever was frustrating them, and get on with things. This follows a normal pattern of adolescent behavior. When an adolescent becomes involved in emotional problems that have harmful effects, the stress level escalates and the lack of prompt recovery is frustratingly evident.

When evaluating stress levels for young people, sources of stress must always be perceptually defined. Stressors are in the eye of the beholder. What is stressful to one person may not be stressful to another. It is a common mistake for adults to assume that what is stressful to us is also stressful to a young person and, conversely, what does not cause us stress should not cause them stress either. This is very often the basis of serious miscommunication between adults and young people.

To illustrate this divergence, consider your feelings about a roller coaster ride in an amusement park. While young people find them to be thrilling and highly attractive, older folks who once found them to be a great source of excitement now view them with abject terror. Another scenario that illustrates this perceptual point of view is the termination of an adolescent relationship. Many adolescents will find the end of a teenage romance to be a crushing experience, while the parents of the adolescent going through this trauma might want to celebrate if they had not approved of the relationship. As a result, one party sees it as traumatic while the other sees it as desirable.

Self-Concept

The sixth psychological aspect to be considered involves the self-concept of the individual. The self-concept is simply a general term describing the way a person feels about himself or herself. One's self-concept can change situationally, it can vary with fatigue and frustration, and it can be affected by a variety of circumstances that occur in one's personal life.

It is clear that young people who experience emotional problems also sustain changes in their self-concept levels. Emotional problems commonly reveal themselves with a simultaneous decline in the self-concept of the individual. There are several ways of looking at the erosion of the self-concept to evaluate its impact on the adolescent.

First, the child or adolescent may hold a generally negative view of himself or herself. This might be expressed in terms of personal criticism often muttered in response to failure, or by a general underestimation of one's ability. A simple compliment, for example, is usually answered by "yeah, but . . ." People who generally respond "yeah, but . . ." to anything that is positive are saying that they do not believe a positive remark is consistent with their level of self-concept.

Second, one's self-concept can be eroding without any communication of its erosion at all. An adolescent struggling with emotional problems will begin to engage in patterns of negative self-talk. This is the internal dialogue that continually goes on in our heads. If we listen carefully we find that we are almost constantly engaging in some banter with ourselves. This conversation may involve what we are doing at the time, it may involve our fantasies, our plans, or our frustrations and sources of depression and anxiety. Too much negativity results in a loss of perspective on a person's self-concept.

Interestingly enough, one can experience a major drop in self-concept levels simply by focusing on patterns of negative self-talk. In many cases parents are bewildered to find their children feeling very badly about themselves when no specific feedback has been given to them to warrant that opinion. Helmstetter (1986) provides a thorough analysis of how self-talk affects the emotional well-being of the individual.

The degree of impact that self-talk has in the life of an adolescent can be informally evaluated. Listen, for example, to the inclination of an individual to exaggerate his or her involvement in things that have gone wrong while underemphasizing his or her responsibility for things that go right. This is a striking symptom of people with negative self-concepts. They can neither accept a positive compliment nor take credit for something that has gone right. However, they nearly always attribute mistakes, errors, and other negative consequences to something they did, said, or in some cases simply thought.

One major consequence of a negative self-concept is a feeling of helplessness. Even when there is no obvious reason to believe otherwise, an adolescent with a negative self-concept will feel unable to act in the face of a problem. This tendency is a major obstacle to helping young people who are involved in Satanic cult activity. They have been so conditioned to believing they are helpless that they cannot leave a cult group even when it may be relatively easy for them to do so.

Finally, the most dangerous implication of negative self-talk is that it allows a person to move toward greater levels of depression. Once the symptoms and self-talk of depression have been mastered, negativity becomes pervasive. If your friends will not confirm your feeling about what a terrible person you are, by proper self-talk you can learn to do it yourself! Maintaining feelings of depression can be done independent of any feedback from friends and family.

Spontaneous Remission

Few psychological signs of trouble are more telling than spontaneous remission, the sudden recovery from a lengthy pattern of emotional problems. Whenever a young person has been perturbed by problems of anxiety, depression, or impulsive behavior for a significant period of time and suddenly reports being "cured," he or she is communicating a matter of serious concern. First, in the evaluation of young people who are suicidal, for example, many therapists have reported that a young person will suddenly appear to have solved all of his or her problems immediately before a suicide attempt. Apparently, the decision to take his or her own life is, for the young person, a great source of relief. Therefore, any young person who has given evidence of self-destructive behavior should be monitored carefully when signs of spontaneous remission are observed. This problem will be further discussed in Chapter 10.

A second aspect of the problem of spontaneous remission relates to involvement in Satanic cults. Young people who have been introduced to Satanic cult activity often find that it represents a timely and pervasive solution to their emotional problems. As a result, their symptoms "disappear." This response to Satanism makes intervention difficult. The difficulty becomes apparent when a therapist attempts to motivate a young person to give up Satanic practices that are a salient cause of relief from emotional problems.

Diffuse Anger

Young people who suddenly are mad at the world, and everyone and everything in it, are experiencing an erosion of their coping abilities.

This inability to cope is accompanied by a general expression of frustration and hostility not connected to a specific source or directed to any object or person. This type of diffuse anger is troublesome to address in a therapeutic setting, as well as frustrating to the relationship between the adolescent and the parents.

Elimination of Guilt

When experienced in proper doses, guilt is an emotion necessary to monitor and improve our behavior. A young person who habitually responds to situations without feeling guilty and who rationalizes feelings of guilt or transforms them into feelings of anger has acquired a serious emotional problem. When feelings of guilt do not follow misbehavior, the motivation to respond constructively to those behaviors is lost. Satanism is an effective means of eliminating guilt feelings.

Reversal of Feelings

Major reversals in emotions are a significant concern to anyone attempting to work with adolescents. For example, a young person insists that certain types of music are distasteful and disgusting and then rapidly takes the opposite position, arguing that it is extremely good music. In another example, a person with previously fairly neutral attitudes and ideas about school will suddenly adopt a strong negative view of school and any associated learning opportunities. These shifts in feelings and emotions are often associated with a sudden pattern of dependency on people, ideas, and practices that are not congruent with the goals of the school or the family. Satanic cult members are encouraged to see parents, for example, as the enemy. It is not so much the fact that negative attitudes exist but the rapid rate of change that is an indicator that something has gone wrong in the emotional life of the adolescent.

Bonding Changes

A common concern in the evaluation of psychological risk factors involves changes in patterns of bonding. Bonding is a term given to patterns of dependency that young people have on adults who serve as role models. When an adolescent suddenly changes patterns of dependency on role models it is often because the new role model is providing for some intense need. When needs are provided for in a negative manner, such as by the introduction to Satanic cults, the bonding to that individual becomes very intense and harmful to the emotional well-being of the adolescent. It is important for parents to know who may be serving as role models in the lives of their children. Any shift or rapid change in role models could indicate a response to an emotional need and could signal the onset of a potential problem.

SOCIAL FACTORS

There are four areas of social interaction that relate to risk profiling: (1) a need for inordinate privacy, (2) extreme parental avoidance, (3) not accounting for money, and (4) anonymous friends. All of these are frequently associated with early stages of cult involvement and, therefore, are important in the early identification of adolescent Satanists.

Needs For Privacy

Most adolescents are covetous of their personal space and will defend their right to privacy. However, they ordinarily do not have intense reactions when their space is occasionally invaded. When a young person is exposed to Satanic cult activities, a strong increase in a need for privacy accompanies that involvement. When an adolescent begins to aggressively assert his or her right to privacy, especially regarding the bedroom, it should be an indication that something has gone awry.

In addition to the privacy regarding personal space, many adolescents who experience emotional problems tend to avoid conversation and feedback from others by acquiring an intense and ongoing interest in music. A young person who spends an inordinate amount of time listening to music with a Walkman-type personal radio or tape player may not be interfering with other people but may be coping with personal problems in a self-defeating manner.

Family Routines

The second area involving social factors is a change in an adolescent's family interaction. This usually begins with the young person spending more time alone while in the house but soon spreads to the avoidance of family activities. An adolescent who repeatedly objects to being a part of family activities may be stating a need to avoid being observed for any length of time. This will allow him or her to engage in activities for which there is no accountability, facilitating involvement in activities that the parent would otherwise prohibit.

Changing Money Habits

Accounting for one's personal money often emerges as a problem when an adolescent becomes involved in Satanism. Young people who suddenly find that they "lose" money without finding it are more likely being very generous with their friends. The pattern of giving money to friends and insisting that it has been lost is a good indication that something is wrong. Parents should insist on accountability for finances. Parents should never accept the argument that a child's personal finances are none of their business. By maintaining their own ignorance, parents enable their children to continue the destructive process of seriously problematic behavior.

Friendship Patterns

Finally, the problem of the "anonymous friend" is one that can have potentially serious implications. A significant change in a young person's behavior regarding friends should be a cause for concern. Most young people will at least briefly introduce parents to friends with whom they socialize. When a young person suddenly talks about having "close friends" but refuses to introduce these friends, parents should be wary. In many cases, these adolescents do not know the names of their new friends, because they are committed to secrecy, as well. Responsible parents are aware of where their children go and what they do together with their friends. These so-called friends maintain their anonymity for good reason, "good reasons" that are also bad for the young person. Parents should be reasonably snoopy, intruding lightly but firmly in a friendly and consistent manner in the lives of young people concerning matters that have to do with their friends.

SUMMARY

Risk assessment is problematic. Parents and mental health workers should be aware that a single symptom does not warrant a conclusion about risk in general. Many children and adolescents will show some of these signs of risk on an occasional basis. However, it requires good judgment and discernment in evaluating these factors—how they cluster and how long they persist—to obtain a valid risk assessment. Persons attempting to assess young people should keep in mind that three factors for evaluating the significance of risk are the frequency, duration, and intensity of symptoms.

How often does the young person manifest signs and symptoms related to risk? The duration of these factors over time should be observed, and the extent to which these characteristics impair the young person's performance in normal life tasks and routines should be determined. Taken together, they give us good clues regarding the ability of young people to resist the problems of Satanism and its destructive influences. With an awareness of these factors we can better assist young people in avoiding problems related to Satanic cult involvement.

4

The Satanic Bible

Most young people who develop an interest in Satanism eventually find their way to the standard book of Satanism, *The Satanic Bible*. This book was first published in 1969 by Anton LaVey, a former circus animal trainer and huckster, as well as the founder of the first Satanic church in the United States. This church still stands in San Francisco with LaVey at its helm.

The Satanic Bible is a collection of essays, most of which argue against the legitimacy of mainstream religion. The remaining essays attempt to explain the basic concepts of what LaVey believes to be the philosophy of Satanism. The final part of his book contains a series of rituals that LaVey suggests be used for the "mastery of the earth." These rituals are cleverly designed to give the illusion of greater power in areas that are most commonly sources of insecurity in the lives of many adolescents. Quite predictably, they emphasize sexual prowess and the ability to control others.

This book has enjoyed a revival in recent years and has become the standard reference for most young Satanists who are eager to learn the alleged craft of the devil. Their eagerness, however, surpasses their thinking skills, leaving them to uncritically accept some rather unusual arguments. LaVey lays the groundwork for the uninformed reader to conclude that Satanism is the only logical choice of religion in contemporary America, the only reasonable religion for a normal, healthy young person. He also implies, of course, that there must be something wrong with anyone inclined to believe otherwise. Addressing a common adolescent insecurity, LaVey argues that embracing Satanism is an affirmation that you are not as disturbed as you or others might think.

Adolescents who are alienated, estranged, and angry at the world are typically vulnerable to anyone who affirms them as acceptable. Preying on their inability to discriminate, LaVey tries to persuade young readers that his philosophy is the only solution to the many problems that confront them. His powerful appeal effectively overcomes the lack of logic and substance of his philosophy. Parents and those who work with young people experiencing emotional difficulties should have a basic understanding of what LaVey has to say in order to address his arguments.

In *The Satanic Bible* LaVey attempts to discredit Christianity by identifying a variety of ideas from mainstream Christianity that are not widely accepted or popular among young people today. In a process of creating a mutually exclusive dichotomy between his philosophy and all religions, LaVey exaggerates the unpopular practices and beliefs of these religions, takes them out of context, and proceeds to reject all Christian religion from this amplified and narrow point of view.

For example, in his discussion of sexuality, LaVey contends that anyone who is a Christian is guilty of lust if he or she experiences "the faintest stirring of sexual desire" (1969, p. 47). This statement seriously distorts any theological or practical position on sexuality and illustrates the style with which LaVey develops contrasts to further support his arguments about the acceptability of Satanism. LaVey's exaggerated claims are followed by the assurance that these stirrings of sexuality are good feelings—healthy, normal experiences—and desirable emotions in the heart of a Satanist. Aren't we all Satanists by this logic?

For the troubled adolescent experiencing difficulty with religiously inspired guilt about sexuality, LaVey's position appears to be extremely attractive, especially when the inescapable conclusion is considered: any experience of one's sexuality is Satanic.

A young reader who has little or no exposure to the theological aspects of his or her religion has little basis upon which to properly evaluate the arguments presented by LaVey. The founder of the Church of Satan did not leave his persuasive skills behind at the circus. He skillfully chose bits and pieces of antiquated theology and wove them into a tapestry of religion that no one could accept. And, if there are only two choices, Satanism is the only acceptable alternative.

To reject his ideas, according to LaVey, implies that there is something wrong with you, or at least something wrong with the way you think. Since most adolescents need affirmation that they are normal, this argument holds great power to sustain their attention.

LaVey enhances his position by frequently describing Satanism as strong and Christianity as weak. To the insecure and disempowered teenager, a position of alleged strength is a powerful attraction. Accepting it makes good sense as long as one also accepts the corresponding argument that other religions represent weakness. An individual's attraction to Satanism, in reality, has little at all to do with religion. It is simply a predictable consequence of living too long with emotional problems that have not been resolved. What today's adolescents need from parents is guidance in dealing with life's problems, not delusions about the existence of problems.

Occult, by precise definition, means hidden. It is the darkness surrounding LaVey that gives him the power he possesses. His ideas are lacking in logic and substance. The mystique of Satan can only exist under the protective shroud of ignorance that blankets the cult believers, as well as many who attempt to positively influence the lives of young people.

LAVEY'S SEVEN MAJOR ASSUMPTIONS

Nearly all of LaVey's philosophy is based on seven major assumptions, none of which are derived from a logical or accurate assessment of contemporary religious belief systems.

Assumption I: Religion and Pleasure Are Mutually Exclusive

The first major assumption of LaVey is the incompatibility between a religious commitment and the enjoyment of life. He argues that anyone who accepts religion as a significant life influence must totally give up all pleasure and enjoyment. A Christian having some fun in life is just not possible, according to LaVey.

We must choose, he claims, between the path of being a religious person and that of being a seeker of pleasure. The gloomy, ascetic life of a religious person is portrayed in bleak and depressing terms. In fact, if we were to take LaVey seriously, only masochists would accept Christianity into their lives. The naive acceptance of this departure from reality is an essential prerequisite for adopting LaVey's Satanism.

Assumption II: Man Is Inherently Violent

LaVey argues that all mankind has a tendency toward violence. He gives a number of examples that would persuade a young, frustrated, and angry reader to believe that violence is hereditary and not learned behavior. When violence is accepted as natural, it follows closely that the use of this "natural violence" is also acceptable, and, in some cases, to be encouraged when it propagates the Satanic belief system and gives more power to its leaders.

Once this idea is established and accepted as true, LaVey encourages the Satanist to strike out against anyone who becomes a problem. He mocks the "turn the other cheek" Christian, exhorting his readers to smash anyone who dares to strike out at them. Rather than viewing anger as one of the seven deadly sins, LaVey argues that we are better off considering anger as necessary to self-preservation and, therefore, natural to our instinctive selves.

This argument is persuasive to the frustrated adolescent who is drawn to *The Satanic Bible* for answers to his or her life problems, especially when these problems are complicated by feelings of diffuse anger. The young person learns a dangerous lesson: pervasive feelings of anger are normal and instinctive. Further, LaVey implies that since they are a normal part of human nature, they cannot be changed. He combines hostility with helplessness, leading a disturbed person to a perilous lack of motivation to try solving these problems. When stripped of the motivation to change problems, the adolescent is left only to justify their existence.

LaVey also argues a theory of innate aggression in humankind, despite the fact that a good deal of anthropological research has concluded otherwise. The definitive and classic study of human aggression conducted by Montagu (1950) concluded that aggression is not innate to the human species. In a later work on social aggression, Bandura (1973) concluded that aggression is learned from the environment and is rewarded by others in that environment. Baron (1985) concludes that we are born with few aggressive responses. We all enter the world with an inherent tendency toward cooperative behavior, and anything that is indicative of aggressive behavior is the result of the frustrations of our natural tendencies. To be aggressive is unnatural, according to Montagu. Therefore, Satanism is equally unnatural.

LaVey insidiously reverses bad to good. Rather than see that aggressive feelings are the result of frustration and failure in life, LaVey persuades the reader to conclude that they must be normal and that everyone feels that way. Finally, he concludes, there is no point in trying to change that which is normal.

Assumption III: Bad and Good Are Reversed

LaVey argues that religion cannot meet the needs of today's young people, and that religion is inherently wrong. Since it is all wrong, LaVey continues, the values it teaches must also be wrong as well. Further, if religion and what it teaches is all bad, it follows that what religion claims to be bad must be good. Through this round of double-talk, LaVey attempts to reverse the semantic meaning of good and bad. For the emotionally troubled adolescent reader, the acceptance of this logic is inviting for two reasons.

First, LaVey allows young people to turn feelings of guilt into a positive emotion. An adolescent exposed to stern and rigid religious upbringing diminishes his guilt completely by accepting LaVey's reversal of good and bad. The relief from guilt feelings is a powerful reinforcer to the adolescent who accepts LaVey's arguments. Consequently, some young people find themselves attracted to Satanism not so much on the basis of its merits, but on the unacceptability of its alternative, that is, religion. Through the manipulation of psychological factors, LaVey exploits the powerful learning process of negative reinforcement to his advantage. In effect, if the reader is not persuaded by the merits of Satanism, he or she will find in it consolation from escaping the intolerable alternative—religion as described by LaVey.

Second, the reversal of good and bad also affects the meanings of messages sent by parents and other well-intended adults to a young cult member. Parents, unaware of this reversal of good and evil, are naturally inclined to plead with the disgruntled adolescent to consider the evil of this decision to become involved with Satanism. Once the adolescent has reversed good and evil, any strategy on the parents' part to attack Satanic philosophy by labeling it as evil is totally counterproductive. It simply encourages further involvement with Satanism, the opposite of what a parent hopes to accomplish.

Assumption IV: Satanism Is Strength

LaVey correctly assumes that young people have a desire and need to be strong and powerful. The fundamental need for power and personal significance drives most people, especially adolescents caught in the midst of personal conflicts. LaVey associates Satanism with the acquisition of power, an association that captures the attention of many young people. All he needs to complete this act of persuasion is to convince the reader that religionists, LaVey's term for Christians, are weak by virtue of their "turn the other cheek" attitude toward others. Instead, he exhorts the reader to "make yourself a terror to your adversary. . . . Thus shall you make yourself respected" (p. 33). He frequently refers to one's enemies, leaving his readers to identify personal enemies as anyone who tries to influence them away from these beliefs.

LaVey probably anticipates that anyone who takes the time to read his book must have enemies against whom the reader is compelled to defend himself or herself. The "us against them" dichotomy furthers the alienation from mainstream society and makes the ideas of Satanism more acceptable.

Assumption V: Satanism Is Now

Satanism, according to LaVey, is the only religion that has any concern for the here and now. He mocks Christians and their view of any meaningful life after death by referring to them as "gazers beyond the grave." LaVey tells the reader that if he or she has any concern for the here and now, Satanism is the only choice. After all, he suggests, Christianity can only deal with the remote future.

Many young people find themselves caught up in impulsive behavior patterns that focus exclusively on the present. These patterns of behavior are typical of young people who are unable to deal constructively with their problems. They are given a justification for ignoring the future and find consolation in their failure to attend to the consequences of their behavior.

Assumption VI: Satanism Is Power

The promise of power through Satanism is central to all of LaVey's arguments. The lure of some acquisition of greater power is the major single attraction of all occult ideas, and it will continue to interest a great number of young people. LaVey literally enchants a young and naive reader with the "Enochian Keys," a long list of ritualistic and rambling prayers to Satan that are supposed to give young Satanists power over others for whatever desire they need to express.

This assumption is so important to LaVey's philosophy that the next chapter is devoted to a greater exploration of this promise of power and how it attracts so many young people to Satanism. There is little question that the interest in Satanism as a source of power is fully dependent on psychologically helpless young people. In reality, the appeal of Satanism is a symptom, masking feelings of helplessness in the face of real life problems. The reasons for these feelings of helplessness will be discussed in the chapter on power.

Assumption VII: We Must Choose between Sex and Religion

LaVey argues that religion and sex are totally incompatible. He makes use of another dichotomy that leads the reader to a forced choice between religion and sexual identity. When expressed in this context, it is unlikely that anyone would forsake all sexual identity to embrace religion. As a result, LaVey makes Satanism out to appear as a matter of logical choice. Nowhere in his book does LaVey give credence to the possibility that an individual can be a religious person and concurrently have a well-defined sense of sexual identity.

Since many adolescents struggle with sexual identity issues, promoting sexual expression as desirable can be especially attractive to a troubled adolescent. LaVey's most insidious statement may be the implication that if you have any sexual feelings you must be a Satanist. Young people who read LaVey's book uncritically and do not question his assumptions are particularly vulnerable to this line of persuasion. Once they read that their sexual emotions or sexual anxieties simply mean they are Satanists, what follows is an enormous sense of relief from the entire constellation of emotional pressures in the area of developing sexual identity that commonly beleaguer so many troubled adolescents.

In the second part of his analysis of sexuality, LaVey devotes an entire chapter to the idea that autoerotic behavior is acceptable and normal activity for an individual. This argument is appealing to a troubled adolescent reader who identifies with this argument in the context of a strict and conservative religious practice that holds masturbation to be sinful and forbidden. Given that masturbation is an experience virtually universal to adolescents, it is understandable that a young reader of *The Satanic Bible* might find consolation in LaVey's arguments, especially if his or her own religious training strictly forbids this sexual experimentation.

The issue for parents is clear. They need to be more understanding of and accepting of the reality that masturbation is common to the adolescent experience. Forbidding this type of sexual experimentation will virtually guarantee that most adolescents will either accept it only marginally or reject it outright. Young people need a religious experience, especially during the difficult time of adolescence. They also need to develop a strong and appropriate sense of sexual identity. Neither one should be forsaken for the other.

The experience of adolescence is universally characterized by an up-surge of sexual drive, and it is simply naive or foolish to deny that this exists. It also follows that a parental attitude toward sexuality as a subject for open and honest discussion is an effective way to ensure that an adolescent will not be unduly persuaded by the arguments presented by LaVey in *The Satanic Bible*.

CONCLUSION

The implications of LaVey's arguments for parents are several. First, a reasonably objective understanding of the principles of Satanism is important for parents to obtain. In knowledge there is power. The knowledge of LaVey's Satanic principles enables parents to understand the process of Satanism and to better recognize the steps through which a young person moves toward greater involvement. In addition, and probably more important, the mystique of Satanism is a major source of power in itself. When Satanic ideas are discussed openly, intelligently, and without confrontation, they lose considerable power in the context of this objectivity. Parents might find these objective questions useful in opening dialogue with their children:

What does power mean to you?

How do you get power?

Can you just feel power, or do you have to do something to get it?

What power comes from helping other people?

The bulk of LaVey's ideas are valued by young people because of their alleged secrecy. Parents should be concerned enough to learn what beliefs attract their children. It is also important that parents show their children that LaVey and other proponents of Satanism have no magic. Their ideas and arguments simply warp logic with clever bits of delusion.

Parents would do well to evaluate the way they teach religion to their children. Religious belief systems that promote an oppressively rigid and narrow perception of morality are more vulnerable to the criticisms leveled by LaVey. A religious practice that includes a concern for one's neighbor and encourages action to promote the betterment of the community has more power than any of the vague Satanic beliefs. This power is enhanced by involvement rather than simply by belief. Power comes to us when we give power to others. This can be experienced in many ways by doing things for people less fortunate than we. It is a powerful experience to empower others.

A young person who experiences the need to take action on the basis of religious convictions and appreciates the outcome of that action learns that religion is a source of significant power in one's personal life. This approach to religion also builds feelings of personal integrity and self-esteem, psychological characteristics notably absent in the development of young people attracted to Satanism.

Third, parents who resort to the manipulation of guilt in their children in the hope of motivating them toward better behavior should carefully reevaluate that practice. The fundamental basis of all of LaVey's arguments is the assumption that we will not separate guilt from religion. Parents who attempt to persuade their children to be more religious by enticing them to feel more guilty may be setting them up for a confrontation with Satanism during adolescence.

Young people who are motivated to comply with parent expectations simply avoid guilt are too dependent to make good decisions. The greater the dependency, the greater the vulnerability to people like LaVey, who prey on weakness, passivity, dependence, and guilt. Parents must recognize that the more that guilt and dependence is fostered in the development of a child, the greater is the resulting vulnerability to Satanic influence and a variety of other self-destructive emotional problems. Parents should ensure that their children are independent and deal only with guilt that is a direct consequence of their behavior.

Finally, we can clearly see that LaVey's intended audience is the growing number of insecure, frustrated, angry, and alienated adolescents who continue to fail in their search for strong and appropriate role models and the experience of good parenting. Our behavior speaks with authority, more so than what we say to adolescents.

Parents who take personal responsibility, who avoid rigidity in religion, who accept appropriate sexuality, and who process guilt in healthy ways will find that their children are highly resistant to adopting belief systems such as those presented by LaVey in his book, *The Satanic Bible*.

5

Satanism as a Source
of Power

Nearly all young people have a normal and healthy need to acquire power and the feelings of confidence that it provides. They will do this in many ways, some good and some bad. The power that accompanies academic achievement, for example, has great reward value for the adolescent. The feelings of confidence and control that accompany this success are fundamental building blocks for a strong ego. Making the football team gives power. So, too, does joining a street gang or becoming the neighborhood bully. Power itself is neither good nor bad. It just gives feelings of significance that tell the young person that he or she matters. Some young people quickly decide that evil power as promised by the Satanist is far more acceptable than a feeling of having no power at all.

Since the pioneering work of Murray (Thetford & Walsh, 1985), most adolescent behavior is explained in the context of meeting needs. The most fundamental adolescent need is to feel a meaningful sense of personal significance and social power, the absence of which leads to alienation, disillusionment, and depression.

Masterson (1985), describing significant emotional problems, coined them the "six psychiatric horsemen of the Apocalypse" and identifies them as depression, fear, anger, guilt, helplessness, and emptiness. He addresses their destructive effect on the personality of the adolescent. The antidote to any one of these psychiatric horsemen is empowerment, and this need for power will drive an adolescent to search the real world for opportunities to acquire personal power. Legitimate sources of power are academic achievement, volunteerism, and athletic prowess, for example.

Urban street gangs provide illegitimate means to the same end. The proliferation of these gang problems in our cities and suburbs is directly related to the lack of positive means for obtaining social power. Cloward and Ohlin (in Gold & Petrino, 1980) describe a theory of "blocked opportunity" to describe how street gangs form. Briefly, Cloward and Ohlin suggest that young people at risk for gang involvement become so because our social structure does not provide them with more legitimate opportunities to obtain these feelings of personal and social empowerment.

When the search of the real world turns up empty, either because of the lack of ability or the lack of opportunity, the promise of power from the surreal world becomes an increasingly viable solution. Veiled in secrecy, ambiguity and its promise of enormous power, the occult world of Satanism becomes an engaging alternative to reality.

OCCULT POWER DEFINED

Our modern world has many examples of occult influence. We are witness to a parade of horoscopes, astrology, tarot, Ouija boards, and the endless magical appellations of spells and incantations found in the media. By definition, the term *occult* has two elements. First, it means something that is not revealed or is hidden from the observer. Second, it implies the possession and utilization of supernormal powers. As a result, the attraction to occult belief systems for most adolescents involves two factors: its hiddenness and its promise of power.

Satanism is a source of power that is promised to serve them if they can learn to understand it. However, this is a big "if." Since most Satanic cult practice entails a pursuit of the unknown, most young people don't know what it is they are supposed to understand. All they know is that it is secret and powerful. Nearly all occult belief systems, and especially Satanism, are based on the assumption that there is something of substance that is unknown. And, if you can figure out what that unknown is, you have obtained a great source of power. This sounds like double-talk, but it explains why so many young people involved in Satanism are unable to articulate exactly what it is they are practicing. While they talk about these vague sources of power they cannot adequately explain, they persist in believing that these powers exist. They are on a search for something without understanding exactly what it is.

PERCEPTUAL POWER

The power promised by Satanism is entirely a matter of perception. However, whether the pursuit of power is an illusion or a reality, the adolescent will behave differently if he thinks he has power. Whether he really does have power or not makes little difference in his behavior. It all depends on what he believes. His behavior is derived entirely from that belief.

To illustrate, suppose you were walking down a dark street in a strange neighborhood at night. If you had any sense at all you would probably feel a little uneasy. You would feel vulnerable to the darkness and to the unknown. Suppose you were carrying a violin case with a powerful weapon in it for your personal protection. You would probably feel a lot more comfortable. The darkness and the unknown would be much less intimidating. In fact, most young people would swagger down that street with an air of arrogance or superiority, knowing full well that anyone getting in their way would be in for trouble.

Suppose, however, this time that you unknowingly picked up the wrong violin case, one that actually contained a violin. So long as you thought you were loaded with power, you would continue to swagger along, projecting an air of confidence and poise that would be obvious to anyone who observed you. The fulfillment of your expectation is, in itself, a source of power.

THE ILLUSION OF POWER

So, what gives the feeling of such security and confidence? Is it a reality or is it an illusion? More importantly, what does it matter? So long as you believe you are powerful and superior, you are what you believe. So it is with Satanism. All you need to have in order to partake of the power of Satan is the belief that you have power. What this power actually is or whether it even exists is relatively inconsequential.

To an adolescent who is struggling with life and fighting off feelings of overwhelming inadequacy and powerlessness, there is not much concern for whether this power source is real or imaginary. In the case of an insecure and frightened adolescent needing power, just about anything will do. The relationship between the need for power and our ability to evaluate power is quite important. The greater the need, the less one is able to evaluate the validity.

In the normal pursuit of power, a connection between sensing a need and actively engaging in a behavior designed to meet that need is necessary for any change to occur. This connection between a perceived need and taking action is often missing for young people who are drawn to occult beliefs. If a child learns that taking action does not result in needs being met, the consequence is a feeling of helplessness. Without a learning history that connects problem solving with the taking of action, the young person is vulnerable to the pursuit of other solutions outside the real world, that is, the world of the metaphysical. When this effort is thought to be successful, it becomes a major obstacle to intervention.

Any parent or counselor who attempts to persuade an adolescent that his or her problems have emerged because of passivity in resolving the problem is in for a challenge. Redirecting inappropriate behavior or shaping maladaptive coping patterns is easier than trying to elicit an initial response from a reluctant adolescent. Changing an adolescent's coping style from passivity to activity is an extremely difficult task if the adolescent has been frustrated by previously failed attempts.

Considering the difficulty of this need to change from a passive approach to an active approach, let's consider how passivity develops in the first place. There is some evidence to suggest that young people learn in childhood to be passive and helpless in the face of problems. This happens when parents do not give their young children consistent opportunities to take specific actions to solve specific problems. Seligman (1975) discusses the serious implications for emotional development that result when people learn to be helpless.

In his work with people who suffer from various problems of depression, Seligman concluded that many adults who have this problem have been raised by parents who responded to them inconsistently. They learned, in effect, to be helpless. Even in the face of obvious evidence to the contrary, these depressed people persisted in the belief that they could not do anything to solve problems. Hence, the term Seligman coined to describe this attitude is "learned helplessness."

Parents need to structure for their young children an environment that provides opportunities to connect the need for a solution with a behavior. An effective way to do this is to respond only to a child when he or she asks for help, and make it a point not to initiate much contact without being asked. In this situation, even a very young child will quickly figure out that his or her request leads to help—an effective lesson in how to control a parent! When a young person has learned early in life that problems require action, it is unlikely that something as vague and passive as Satanism will be of any great attraction to them.

Why do so many young people feel so powerless that they fall victim to the lure of Satanism and its promise of great power? We need to take a closer look at some of the implications of power and how it becomes a dominant force, and occasionally an obsession, in so many lives.

First, it is important to understand that power is a basic need upon which our very survival depends. Nearly every behavior a child engages in can be interpreted as an attempt to master the environment, that is, to obtain power. Children will do this in a wide variety of ways, some of which are realistic and productive, others less so. Younger children, when they engage in play activities, often compete aggressively for positions of authority and control. It should be no surprise to see that toys representing power have a dominant role in play activities for young children, especially boys.

There are also a wide variety of fantasies that promote and lend expression to our instinctive fascination with power. These are often seen in the entertainment industry. For example, the popularity of movies with heroic figures such as Batman and Superman have common elements, all portraying fantasy representations of men of incredible power.

In the real world we can observe the pursuit of power dominating politics. The positions of power in the world today are sought after by many people, some of whom would do literally anything to obtain that power. Finally, young people who are drawn to street gangs and the proliferation of weapons associated with these gangs are often those who feel the most powerless in our society and our culture. They are struggling to compensate for these perceived feelings of powerlessness by acquiring weapons and becoming gang members.

In light of these factors it should be clear that we have a serious responsibility to empower children. This responsibility belongs primarily to parents, but is also a central concern to teachers, mental health workers, and other people involved with working with children.

DEVELOPMENTAL ASPECTS OF POWER

If we take a brief excursion into the world of the child it becomes apparent how the power quest becomes so ingrained. One of the most common problems in child and adolescent behavior involves the difficulty that young people have in accepting their meager dole of power in the world. Many young adolescents become so tangled up in fantasies about power and its expression through sexual prowess and violence that they are unaware of the realistic consequences of these pursuits, such as unwanted pregnancies or going to prison.

Elements of the need for power are present at birth. Child psychologists describe the infant as having a primitive perception of being the most powerful person in the world. The infant cannot distinguish between himself or herself and the mother. Anything in the environment is believed to be in the control of, or caused by, his or her primitive actions. Freud called this "primary narcissism," the faulty belief of having more power than you really possess. This primitive little mind of the infant is in store for a rude awakening; infants are not powerful at all. In fact, they are helpless creatures initially dependent on others for everything.

SATANISM AND POWER NEEDS

Satanism and its promise of power can be a potent attraction to a young person. Parents who do not respond to their child's needs for empowerment are likely to encourage feelings of powerlessness that lead the young person to compulsively and implicitly accept promises of power. Parents' responses to a child's behavior and misbehavior must be consistent enough so that the child learns that certain behaviors gain certain advantages. If a child wants to be praised, he or she knows what to do, and when a child wants to avoid being punished, he or she also knows exactly what not to do. When these messages get mixed and twisted in the experience of the young child, the consequences are potentially catastrophic.

It is, therefore, an important responsibility for parents to allow the young child to have consistent and gradually increasing experiences of power. The hallmark of good mental health is an ability to have an effect in the real world. Commonly, the ability to make things happen only in a fantasy world is an indication that something has gone wrong in the life of the child.

Although it may appear that the major task in early childhood is to accept this state of helplessness and learn to be comfortable depending on others, this is not true at all. In fact, just the opposite is true. Normal and healthy babies struggle constantly for a sense of gaining control of their world. This quest for control will put a child in some difficult situations, as any parent well knows. Healthy young children, in the exploration of their environment, seem forever to be trying things that can be dangerous, going places that could be risky, and testing the limits of their control and power, as well as the patience of the parent.

Learning to deal with having little power and subsequent attempts to obtain power constitute the major developmental task of childhood. This struggle continues on into adolescence, as well. In fact, we might reasonably agree that a definition of responsible adulthood would be the comfortable acceptance and proper use of one's power.

Exposure to a destructive environment that does not nurture feelings of power simply makes a child more vulnerable to the lure of Satanism and its promise of power. Satanism will meet the power needs of a young person in three ways.

First, many adolescents involved in Satanism are extremely deceptive. They, in fact, are led to conclude that their ability to deceive other people, especially their parents, is good evidence of Satan working in their lives and therefore giving them greater power. As an aside, it is also interesting to note that some parents of young people who become involved in Satanism have serious problems in their denial of what is happening. The parents' denial is interpreted by the adolescent as a sign of greater power of deception and is attributed to the work of Satan, and thereby inadvertently contributes to the problem.

Second, a great deal of the practice of Satanism is conducted under a veil of secrecy. The claim of secret knowledge is a source of power in itself. Many young people will insist that they know something that you do not understand. As a result, they are given a feeling of greater empowerment in this claim of superior knowledge and secret rituals.

Third, the most insidious use of power involves the taking of one's life. In some cases people who become involved in Satanism with preexisting suicidal thought patterns will find that occult behavior facilitates the development of these thought patterns, giving a sense of greater power over one's own life. This is occasionally seen in an extremely disturbed youngster who becomes involved in Satanic activity and uses the cult beliefs to justify the act of suicide. It is apparent that the ritualistic abuse of oneself, of others, and of animals in the practice of Satanism is a source of power for those who become involved. The act of dominating, controlling, and abusing people in a perverse way effectively satisfies a disturbed person's need for power.

These lures of power are only significant to the person who has intense and preexisting feelings of powerlessness. The need to acquire power through occult activities is driven by a desire to assuage these intense feelings of powerlessness. This is exactly where parents must intervene preventively to ensure that Satanism is not taken seriously in adolescence.

CONCLUSION

A final comment on the nature of power is that it is unique to the individual. What might give one person power may not be of any significance to another. The perceptual nature of power for a young person is an important concept in our understanding of what empowers them. Remember also that young people often find power in activities that may be of little significance to us. Household responsibilities appropriate to the age of the child are an excellent example. Our attempts to empower young people will be successful only if we provide significant experiences enabling them to feel that their actions have a positive effect. These activities should include prescribing a role in the family that leaves children with a valid feeling that their contributions make a difference. Recently I discussed this with a colleague who stated that she played an absolutely critical role in her family during childhood. She milked the cows! Some families need more cows.

6

The Satan-God Duality

Dualities exist in every area of human endeavor. A duality, by definition, involves two opposites, each giving greater meaning to the other.
Our present culture and cultures before ours have literally evolved within
a dualistic framework. Examples of cultural dualities can be observed
throughout the world. In the Australian aboriginal culture we find the
sacred-profane contract (Yengoyan, 1989) inexorably linking good with
evil, each pole enhancing the meaning and understanding of the other.
In the Indonesian culture, similar dual structures are also prevalent (Fox,
1989). In the African Irigwe tribe, dualities form the core of their perceptions of good and evil. Twins born into this tribe are seen as one
good and one evil. The latter, once determined, is killed (Sangree, 1971).
Dualities are found in nearly all anthropological studies of world culture
(Maybury-Lewis & Almagor, 1989).

DUALITIES IN PHILOSOPHY

Dualities are philosophically essential to the work of Hegel. In his
writings we find a process of growth that has come to be known as
dialectical idealism. Each idea, a thesis, has a corresponding opposite,
the antithesis. Change, growth, or the advancement of knowledge is
found in the synthesis of these contrasting ideas. This dialectic can be

found in the works of Socrates, whose Socratic method involves questions posed to the learner from opposing points of view. In the political arena, the concept of the dialectic is basic to the works of Marx and others who envisioned a new order arising from the synthesis of existing dualities (Russell, 1945). This is, for example, the basis of most radical political thought. If you can promote an extreme alternative to the prevailing order, a compromise will give you greater political gain.

DUALITIES AND LANGUAGE

In addition, the development of language relies heavily on the meaning of dualities to enrich the impact of communication. In the English language, for example, we see dualities provide meaning to many events common to our lives. Right is understood as a contrast to what is wrong. Night gives meaning to day. These dualities stand in contrast to each other. They sharpen and clarify our conceptualization about the meaning of things in the world. Our social interactions are marked by the use of dualities in everyday conversation. For example, you may have heard this attempt to describe a Democrat: "Well, he's not a Republican, after all." Or perhaps this account of how a person survived an accident: "She's not dead, at least." Or, "Did you enjoy your last dinner at this restaurant?" "Well, it wasn't bad." We rely on such dualities to communicate ideas we are attempting to effectively convey to another person. Dualities give a background that more clearly frames many ideas we communicate to others. Yengoyan (1989) argues that these dualistic principles operate within the semantic domain of all language. They are fundamental to brain functioning.

DUALITY AND DEATH

Some philosophers insist that we cannot appreciate the true value of life without giving serious thought to death. If you want to appreciate being alive, think awhile about being dead. Koestenbaum (1971) suggests that the vitality of life is derived from a contemplation of our own death. May, Angel, and Ellenberger point out "the fact that non-being is an inseparable part of being. To grasp what it means to exist, one needs to grasp the fact that he might not exist" (1958, p. 47). We will see later that this line of reasoning can be seriously distorted for some young people who dabble in Satanism. They can twist these ideas into a justification for suicide.

THE DUALITY OF GOOD AND EVIL

Furthering our pursuit of the dualistic nature of the world, it follows that the nature of good cannot be fully understood without an opposing concept of evil. This has been the subject of much philosophical discussion. The dance of meaning between good and evil serves as an individual dialectic that forms the substance of human evolution intellectually, ethically, morally, and spiritually. Gray (1989) argues that the concept of good has no meaning without equal status accorded to evil. Each, he says, makes the existence of the other both believable and meaningful. Jung suggests that the nature of a good-evil duality is basic: "Every good quality has its bad side, and nothing good can come into the world without at once producing a corresponding evil" (1971, p. 459).

This polarity of good and evil, according to Kekes (1988), is essential to the understanding of human nature. From a Jungian perspective this duality is also an integral part of the unconscious dimension of the human condition (Jung, 1971). A common manifestation of this unconscious duality is found in the rituals of the compulsive neurotic, whose patterns of behavior involve doing and undoing. The formation of most patterns of compulsive behavior involves dualities that are known to the person who practices them in a frantic search for relief from anxiety (Cameron, 1963).

Human nature is woven into a dualistic framework. The consideration of a deity is not exempt from the pervasive nature of dualities. As early as the third century, the Manichaeans taught that there were two eternal and contrasting principles of creation, one good and one evil (Balducci, 1990). The medieval religious sect, the Cathars, proposed a concept of God that had a major impact on twelfth-century Europe. They believed that an ultimate evil was a reality, and its embodiment was Lucifer, believed to be a second son of God, a brother to Christ (Russell, 1988).

THE ANTICHRIST: SATAN

Think about your personal conceptualization of God, for example. You probably would find your concept incomplete without using a duality: "The total opposite of evil," for example. The implication is clear:

our concept of God introduces Satan to our thinking, and for many people it is a necessary duality that gives a fuller and richer appreciation to a personal conceptualization of God.

Jung (1959) describes Satan as the Antichrist, the embodiment of the opposite of God. The concept of Antichrist also serves to represent the dark side of human existence. The Antichrist represents those aspects of the human spirit that nurture a part of our personality attracted to the world of sinful pleasure and the pursuit of evil.

Our concept of God has since been associated with an awareness of the devil and his cohorts. The more we contemplate God, the longer an image of Satan must stand in contrast, to complete a dialectic of the deity. While some religions, the Jewish tradition, for example, pay this little mind, other religious sects exploit this dialectic by using reverse psychology. Rather than the worship of God, they promote a fear of the devil to literally scare the hell out of their congregation. In short, the followers do not walk toward God, they back away from the devil. For some, this evangelistic pounding on the fear of Satan has backfired. What was most feared has become attractive to the troubled adolescent who opposes everything in authority. Adolescence is a time for oppositional behavior patterns to emerge. These young people gravitate to the opposite of what authority tells them to do. Most of this acting out diminishes with maturity. For some, an attraction to Satan as a form of oppositional behavior becomes the norm.

There is mention of Satan in the traditional Christian religion as early as the second century (Russell, 1988). Here we find a story of Satan who initiated heaven's great civil war. In his rebellion against God, Satan was cast out of heaven by Michael the Archangel and relegated to hell for the duration of eternity. Taking advantage of this story, many early churchmen promulgated the belief that you cannot serve two masters; if you do not obey the clergy, you must be worshiping the devil. This idea provided a justification for the Crusades as well as for the Inquisitions that terrorized much of medieval Europe.

Satan has not lost favor in contemporary religious thinking either. In the Roman Catholic Church, for example, there is a growing number of clergymen who believe that Satan is more active than ever. They report an increase in the number of cases of demonic possession in the past few years. In his interview with a Roman Catholic exorcist, Stefano Paci (1990) reported that "the number of cases of possession in the West has reached alarming levels." This exorcist, Balducci (1990), argues passionately that Satan is alive and well, so well, in fact, that there are great numbers of devils in the world today and it is a serious theological and practical error to deny their existence because denial enables their evil work to continue.

A common atheistic concept of Satan's influence, one that describes him as an attitude rather than a person, has been proposed by Anton LaVey in his 1969 book, *The Satanic Bible*. In this work, LaVey describes Satan not as an individual, but as an attitude that promotes the pleasures of life, especially those that involve sexual acting out. In Chapter 4 we saw LaVey argue for an attitude that is antithetical to what he thinks is the prevailing Christian attitude toward life and the practice of religion. As a result, he exploits a duality of attitudes. Satanism, according to LaVey's writing, involves the worship of pleasures that are forbidden by traditional Christian religions. LaVey's ideas are important to a fuller understanding of Satanism.

The representation of the devil in whatever form, however, is less important to our understanding of Satanism. What really matters is the psychology behind these images and the reasons young people become drawn to them. If we can more precisely and more objectively understand Satanism and how its influence spreads among young people, we are led to the conclusion that its seeds of influence are planted in the mind of the child very early in life. With a more thorough assessment of the styles of interaction between children and their parents we begin to understand the factors that predispose adolescents to a greater vulnerability to Satanism.

THE DUALITY OF HEAVEN AND HELL

Duality also lends greater clarity to our thinking about heaven and hell. Pleasure, contentment, and happiness is expected by most members of the Christian faith when they go to "heaven" after death. This idea can be more greatly appreciated by contrasting it with the hellish alternative. We gain a more appropriate appreciation for heaven by thinking about hell. As a result, many people are motivated to get to heaven because the fires of hell are believed to be so damned hot. In the psychology of learning, this is known as negative reinforcement, an effective motivator of human behavior. The individual is not primarily trying to move toward a positive alternative; he or she is more highly motivated to get away from a distasteful situation. We can be motivated in our religion by one of two ways: to seek God because we love God, or to seek God only because we fear the possibility of an encounter with Satan.

THE EXPLOITATION OF DUALITIES

Proponents of some religions make a serious mistake in their exploitation of the concept of duality. An effective religion, in the mind of an adolescent, must focus on the desirability of being with God and shift focus away from the worry of avoiding Satan. In my clinical experience, I have found that manipulating fear simply does not work to motivate an adolescent to do anything productive, especially to practice religion.

A common theme of adolescent behavior, especially for those who are experiencing emotional difficulty, involves opposition to ideas, beliefs, and values that are held by the parent. If the parent holds a view of religion that exploits dualities, the adolescent is likely to adopt ideas congruent with Satanism as an expression of opposition to adult religious values. Adolescents who act out with behaviors that are in opposition to their parents usually do not discriminate very well. As a result, it is not uncommon to see all parent values rejected during this time of rebellion. The concept of Satanism is attractive in this regard because it encourages the adolescent to reject all ideas about attendant morality and other values that accompany this view of religion.

Although dualities are essential to understanding basic elements of our world, it is apparent that they are not without their problems. Many adolescents go through a relatively predictable process of oppositional behavior. This is a normal phase of adolescent development. Basically, most oppositional behavior involves an adolescent's need to assert independence from parents. The adolescent who takes the opposite point of view from the ideas, attitudes, and values of a parent is attempting to assert an independent sense of identity. Oppositional behavior is commonly associated with adolescence since a major developmental task of adolescents is to define a clearer sense of who they are, independent of parents and other adults.

Adolescents engaged in oppositional behavior are often more rigid and inflexible in their thinking. Combs and Snygg (1959) describe the problems that result from this rigidity. Troubled young people have greater difficulty looking at shades of gray that exist between black and white. They often find themselves caught taking one position or its opposite, unable to feel comfortable without the closure and security afforded by clinging to an extreme belief.

A serious problem can result for the adolescent when dichotomous thinking becomes the means by which he or she views theology and organized religion. The practice of religion and belief in God becomes an all-or-none proposition. It becomes an especially difficult problem when an adolescent begins to question, as many do, his or her perceptions and beliefs about God. In these cases it is likely that the dichotomous thinking will lead the individual to search for the opposite of God as a logical solution to feelings of rebellion against religion.

A second point about the nature of duality is essential to the understanding of adolescent Satanic cult behavior. While most of the thinking about dualities relates to general concepts existing in the world, external to ourselves, the influence of dualities can be found in our highly personal thinking process about ourselves, as well.

As we discussed earlier, we tend to use dichotomies, such as right-wrong, good-bad, and so on, to more sharply clarify our own personal thinking process. In fact, as we become more vulnerable to the impact of stress and frustrations in our private lives, the more we tend to rely on these dichotomies to maintain control of our feelings and thoughts. In troubled marriages, for example, it is common to hear one or both parties describe the other in totally negative terms, unable to discern personal strengths and weaknesses in any relative balance.

For some young people, frustrations and anxieties cannot be otherwise managed or controlled except by interpreting everything in a dichotomous manner. If this artificial categorization cannot be done, the idea is intolerable and rejected, not on the merits of the idea, but on the basis of the fact that the dichotomous mind does not easily tolerate thinking that does not fit neatly into one of only two categories. For example, the family, school, politics, and other institutions of the general society are seen by most people as having a mix of positive and negative characteristics. Young people who are primed to think dichotomously by their personal stress and frustration will usually see these institutions as all bad or they will simply reject them outright. Young people often look at their friends from this perspective, either defending them blindly, or avoiding them altogether.

The tendency of adolescents to think in dichotomous terms exposes them to greater vulnerability when ideas are presented dualistically. As we saw in Chapter 4, the evaluation of *The Satanic Bible,* much of the writing on Satanism is styled in a manner that creates artificial dichotomies, making the rejection of mainstream religion and family values an attractive alternative. The adolescent process of dichotomous thinking lines up with the hucksterism of these occult dualities.

The adolescent rejection of parental religious values is the first of a two-step process. This act of rejection is really a matter of transferring their allegiance from one value system to another. Most adolescents are unaware that their disengagement from parental and religious values results, by default, in the acceptance of another system of values. The nature of that new value system is potentially the source of serious emotional problems for some young people. The need to define a sense of identity blinds the individual to the negative consequences of an oppositional behavior style. These adolescents focus on the rejecting much more clearly than on the new values they are adopting by default.

In exactly the same manner as the rejection of Satan leads to the acceptance of God for a convert to Christianity, the rejection of God leads to the acceptance of Satan for the impulsive and acting-out adolescent who is in the midst of an oppositional period of emotional development.

CONCLUSION

The need for opposition, dichotomous thinking, and the duality of God and Satan place some adolescents in a vulnerable position. These dualities form a web of psychic tension, the escape from which is Satanism (Moriarty & Story, 1990). No wonder some young people embrace Satanism as a global solution to the psychic tension caused by these three spheres of influence. Satanism as a solution emerges by default rather than by design. It is often not the belief of choice but, rather, the consequence of one's need to fill the void created by the rejection of currently held and long-embraced values of religion and the family. What makes the value system of Satanism so insidious for vulnerable young people is how it diminishes the discontent encountered by the troubled adolescent in the search for a sense of personal identity.

7

Rites of Passage

The increase of interest in Satanism by young Americans is evident from a number of sources. We have seen increasing attention paid to this problem in the popular press as well as in professional literature. There is also a growing number of self-professed "experts" traveling the lecture circuit who are more than happy to take your money and literally scare the hell out of you with their horror stories about how Satan is taking over the world. The emotionally intensified response to this literature and these speakers show that interest in Satanism continues to grow.

Some regard Satanism as a religious issue that should be resolved by members of religious organizations when it becomes a problem in the life of an individual. After all, they reason, it is a problem of perverted spirituality. Others, however, have tended to dismiss problems related to Satanism as part of a passing fad that will be outgrown by rebellious adolescents. Neither of these responses, however, works very well.

Despite the clergy's response to Satanism, it continues to be a problem. And, despite efforts by many to ignore the issue, it continues to exist. Parents, schools, law enforcement, the mental health community, and others interested in helping young people cannot ignore this phenomenon.

Although current books are available that explain the general aspects of Satanism, there is little available to explain why Satanism has, in recent years, become attractive to young people. In this chapter we will explore the ways in which our modern culture ignores the traditional adolescent rite of passage, leaving today's adolescent more vulnerable to the influence of Satanic cult belief systems. First, let us consider the cultural role played by adolescent rites of passage.

THE ROLE OF RITUAL

Rituals typically conjure up images of authority, power, and carefully prescribed rules of conduct. In Christian religions, especially the Roman Catholic faith, rites of passage are reminiscent of any of the meticulously prescribed religious ceremonies that have served as spiritual landmarks for the major periods of transition in our lives. For most Christians these transition periods are ceremoniously greeted with a sacrament. In fact, the word given to these rites of passage, sacrament, is derived from the Latin word *sacrare,* meaning to consecrate. These rituals are not taken lightly by the faithful. They are literally sacred, the most sacred of which is the ritual of the Roman Catholic Mass (Murphy, 1979).

Lefevre (1989), writing for the *National Catholic Reporter,* concluded that a disproportionate number of Catholics are involved in cults today. She estimates that most cults, both Satanic and religious, are made up of about 40 percent Catholics. Lefevere also quotes a priest, Fr. James LeBar, who questions the effectiveness of the Catholic rite of confirmation, saying that it does not do what it is supposed to do, that is, to introduce young people to a mature practice of religion in adulthood. Presumably confirmation, as prescribed by the church, serves as an inoculation against the influence of cult attraction.

Most Christians avail themselves of at least four major sacraments, each experienced at a major transition in life. One is born into the world of Christianity by baptism, becomes an adult by confirmation, and leaves the family to begin a separate life through marriage. Finally, the Christian leaves this life comforted by the last rites. Death rituals are common to many cultures. They serve to provide us with an understanding of our own death (Myerhoff, 1982).

The fact that we use sacraments to assist during major transitions in our lives suggests that we may be more vulnerable during times of major change. Rituals offer protection. They are responsive to our vulnerability to personal danger and the forces of evil. Horton describes the role of ritual as a "means of discovering the constant principles that underlie the apparent chaos and flux of sensory experience'' (in Burns & Laughlin, 1979).

Rites of passage are by no means restricted to religious events in our lives. Anyone who has pledged a fraternity or sorority in college will attest to the ritualistic nature of that experience. Many social organizations such as the Knights of Columbus or the Masons employ elaborate rites of passage for induction into their membership. Our society also provides rituals for transitional experiences in our lives. Codifying marriage laws is a secular equivalent to the sacrament of marriage in the church. Bureaus of vital statistics are responsible for recording events of birth, marriage, and death. Roberts (1988) discusses the role of rituals as markers for life transitions in many cultures.

Many other cultures, often referred to as "primitive," that is, having long withstood the test of time, place a high value on the ritualistic greeting of major life transitions. These involve birth, adulthood, marriage, and death. In many cultures, for example, we find that rites of passage are essential to the preservation of these societies. These practices bind its members into a carefully prescribed code of conduct that do not allow for individual expression. As a result, the values and mores of the culture are handed down through generations with little opportunity for change. Turner (1982) and his colleagues have surveyed the role of ritual in various cultures throughout the world.

There is one significant distinguishing characteristic between these groups and our contemporary society. We do not typically honor adolescent rites of passage, while so-called primitive societies place a high value on the experience of becoming an adult. We have left adolescents to figure out this challenge with no ritualistic aid. Nevertheless, most psychologists would agree with the anthropologist Myerhoff, who concludes, "There is every reason to believe that rites of passage are as important now as they have always been, for our social and psychological well-being" (1982, p. 129). Today's adolescent is left to his or her own devices to experience the major life transition from childhood to adulthood. Such transitions are periods of emotional and spiritual vulnerability. In today's society this period of life has become extremely hazardous and has reached a degree of complexity that far exceeds the transitions of previous generations. Opportunities to fail as well as to succeed are more available than in previous generations. For example, the uncertainty of a compelling rate of change in our society requires that many young people prepare themselves for careers that do not yet exist. Drugs, gangs, AIDS, and suicide are all paths to destruction that were little known to previous generations.

FIVE PURPOSES OF RITUALS

Campbell, in his important work, *The Power of Myth* (1988), suggests that rites of passage serve at least five major roles for the adolescent in any culture. First, they establish the balance between mind and body. Second, they provide a prescribed encounter with fear. Third, rites of passage define the boy's role as the father's son, thereby conferring on the father a responsibility for propagating young adult values. Fourth, Campbell discusses rituals of transition to adulthood as necessary to our acceptance of a code of behavior for adults in the society. Finally, he suggests that the adolescent rite of passage provides the adolescent with a first glimpse of death. Through the rite of passage, the adolescent first comes to accept his or her mortality.

The ideas proposed by Campbell create a fascinating view of the transition between the world of the child and the world of an adult. Satanism, on the other hand, is a serious consequence of one's failure to make this transition successfully. A closer look at the roles described by Campbell will provide us with a greater awareness of the value of and need for ritual in the life of the adolescent.

Body-Mind Balance

Children typically place a high priority on physical prowess. Anyone who has observed a group of young boys at a school recess, for example, will agree that physical activity is a high priority of most boys. For some, this becomes an inordinate preoccupation and source of power. We call them bullies. A difficult adjustment to adulthood lies ahead for a young adult who has not properly balanced the powers of the body with the powers of the mind. Young adults who rely on their physical prowess soon find that this is a short-lived means to success in life.

Survival in our society cannot happen mindlessly. The increasing complexity of our technology demands the restoration of this balance between body and mind as an essential prerequisite to survival. Simply stated, we must accept the reality that both of these dimensions are essential to success and longevity. When this balance is not struck, the pursuit of power is a higher priority than what our society can properly address. Consequently, the pursuit of power is displaced to other activities, outside the proper domain of accepted activities in our society. Imber-Black, Whiting, and Roberts (1988) describe a major purpose of ritual as that of incorporating both sides of a contradiction. As a result, rituals provide security and consolation in a world that often does not make sense.

Transcending Fear

The second role of the adolescent rite of passage involves the need to overcome fear. Adolescence is a frightening time of life for many young people. Increased sexuality, the awkwardness of rapid growth, and the greater intensity and complexity of social relationships all serve to make the period of adolescence one of trepidation for many young people.

We also know that many adolescents, especially males, are not likely to admit to their feelings of fear. The adolescent mind commonly equates fear with weakness and is, therefore, more inclined to deny those feelings rather than admit to them and attempt to overcome them. The result of this coping pattern is often a display of behavior that is driven by repressed fear. These feelings are commonly expressed backhandedly through reckless behavior, dangerous and apparently frightening to an observer, yet serving a purpose. Hinsie and Campbell (1974) refer to these reckless actions as counterphobic behavior, an attempt to master anxiety by repeatedly coping with danger. This style of coping with fear is described by Cameron (1963) as reactive courage. He describes reactive courage as common to adolescents who seek out fearful situations because of a need to master the anxiety produced by fear. The more a young person is anxiety-ridden, the greater the likelihood that counterphobic behavior and reactive courage will be employed as a solution to that anxiety.

There are other means of dealing with repressed anxiety and fear. In a clinical setting, we often see various forms of escapism such as drug and alcohol abuse commonly used by young people who mismanage their feelings of fear.

Rites of passage, on one hand, provide a valuable service to an adolescent by giving a structured opportunity to overcome these fears. Rituals provide a sense of control over an intimidating world, serving as a glue to hold things together. On the other hand, as a substitute for this ritual experience, Satanism can serve as a vehicle for relieving a troubled mind of irrational fears. In fact, its biggest attraction is the promise of power, an antidote to problems of repressed fear. In addition, the use of drugs and alcohol almost always accompanies involvement in Satanic cult activities, furthering the escapist value of the experience. We will see in Chapter 10 that suicide, the ultimate form of escapism, is thought to be an act of courage by some Satanists.

Conferring the Father's Role

A common problem particularly associated with adolescent male development is the declining number of good role models available to them. All children have a significant developmental need for exposure to a role model in order to fully understand what they are to become and to see by example the roles properly enacted by adults in our society. The consequences of our failure to provide children with good role models as they approach adolescence can lead to developmental problems that add to the difficulty of growing up. Such neglect can even lead to the destruction of valuable potential in young lives. This issue has been the subject of a vast amount of research that is well-summarized by Lamb (1981).

Most adolescents, male or female, when deprived of a role model, will seek one out on their own. Our society, with its inordinate value placed on sports heroes and music and entertainment stars, aggressively presents a variety of substitute role models to our young people. Some of these are healthy substitutes. Others flaunt a lifestyle that flagrantly rejects the dominant values of our society. In *The Satanic Bible,* for example, LaVey describes Satan as a model of deportment, one whose behavior should be imitated.

Prescribing Rules of Conduct

Rites of passage also prescribe rules of conduct. They resolve contradictions and provide support for strong emotions (Imber-Black, Roberts, & Whiting, 1988). We learn to act like an adult by the experience of these rites of passage if they are made available to us. Campbell has concluded that any society without proper rituals has, in effect, left its young people without the necessary guidelines to behave in a civilized society. He also argues that our abandonment of rituals has included the abandonment of rules of order. Without properly conceived rites of passage, young people simply do not know how to conduct themselves in contemporary society.

Without this psychological anchoring, young people float from one attraction to another, lacking a positive value system or appropriate model of behavior to fill the void created by the loss of ritual. There is greater appeal to Myerhoff's suggestion that we create rituals for ourselves in order to obtain their psychological value. In this essay, she notes prophetically that "the actual doing of a ritual for oneself or another, is often quite frightening, then exhilarating" (1982, p. 131). Satanism offers to fill the void by providing the adolescent with rituals that are indeed frightening and exhilarating, but it also promises power with its carefully prescribed rules of conduct. In this process of becoming attracted to the ritualistic practices of Satanism, young people aspiring to greater freedom really are controlled by new rules of behavior. They lose freedom in the process and have come to serve another master, one who has little concern for their personal welfare.

Acceptance of Death

Finally, rites of passage help us accept that just as surely as life begins, it will end. Van Gennep (1960) describes the mourner in the ritual of the funeral rite as situated between the world of the living and the world of the dead. Children, however, rarely contemplate the fact that life is temporary. When they do, the result is often a glamorous conception of death that does not square with reality. Adults, mature ones at least, have a different perspective.

The inevitability of death, according to thanatologist Koestenbaum (1971), gives meaning and vitality to life. In our acceptance of death we learn to live. Proper rites of passage provide this perspective to the adolescent as he or she assumes the responsibilities of adult life. A common feature associated with adolescent suicide is the fact that its victims have naive and often glamorous views of their own death.

Satanism also provides a perspective on death, one that is seriously distorted and that tempts the young person to develop a fascination with death and view death as a source of power in itself rather than as a backdrop to the power of life.

ADOLESCENCE: THE MISSING RITUAL

Rites of passage serve a valuable role in many cultures. As we consider the impact of these rituals on our current society we see that birth, marriage, and death are assisted by sanctioned rituals. The fourth period of transition, becoming an adult, is conspicuously absent today. Apparently we can be born, get married, and die with the full support of rituals provided by society and religion. In becoming an adult, however, we are left to our own devices. Herein lies a serious problem for many young people.

The failure to provide ritualistic aid for the entry into adulthood has created a psychological and a social void. Regardless, however, the transition will inevitably occur. Boys will become men and girls will become women. Whatever assistance needed in the process will be obtained; if not found within the values of society, it will be found outside the standards traditionally espoused by our culture.

Within the context of most rites of passage one finds two major developmental tasks addressed. First, in leaving the world of childhood, the individual is given a clear point in time from which it is no longer appropriate to embrace the trappings and activities of the child. Second, the ritual serves to mark the beginning of one's membership in adult society. It is both the clarity of these rituals and their social acceptance that helps to develop the young adult's sense of personal identity.

These rituals play an important role in the prevention of many adolescent problems related to estrangement, alienation, and other difficulties commonly associated with the adolescent's task of developing a sense of identity. According to Erikson (1968), a major developmental task of adolescents involves finding a lifelong answer to the question, "Who am I?" The use of cultural rites of passage clarifies the answer to this question. He or she is a child until the rite of passage, after which time there is no confusion in the mind of any of society's members that adulthood has begun for the individual. The individual knows where he or she stands relative to the expectations of the society. There are no mixed messages.

These rites of passage have two fundamental dimensions. First, they provide a process of emancipation from previous dependency relationships common to childhood. Separation from the ways of the child is achieved in a manner that is clear to everyone. Second, they serve as a formal entry into the adult world and establish conditions necessary for assuming an adult identity. Both dimensions of this rite of passage must be present in order to meet the developmental need for adolescent emancipation. In many cultures outside of our own, this job is done in a very efficient manner by tightly prescribed rituals.

Today we have neglected to provide our adolescents with rites of passage that adequately meet both dimensions of the task. As a result, too many young people are left not knowing where they stand in our society. Our modern culture is of little assistance in providing young people with an answer to the question of "Who am I?" The adolescent is often left without guidance to resolve questions related to the task of identity. Many adolescents are on their own to wonder if they are children, if they are adults, or if they belong somewhere in between. With no clear definition of childhood, of adolescence, or even of adulthood, we have effectively stranded many young people in their search for answers to questions regarding their sense of personal identity and how they fit into our culture.

COUNTERCULTURAL RITUALS

In light of this, it is no surprise to see countercultural rituals emerge and begin to assume an important role in the lives of adolescents. When the culture provides no rite of passage, the adolescent is often forced to create one within the framework of a negative contextual structure. In other words, the absence of a cultural rite of passage does not eliminate the psychological need for ritual. It simply deprives an adolescent of one source of assistance and emotional support when it is needed. These times are commonly marked by emotional conflict and resulting stress and, given the degree of turmoil, the need for ritual becomes increasingly more important to the adolescent. When these rituals are not provided by our culture, a young person will seek out substitute rites of passage. When left to their own devices to determine these rituals, many adolescents look toward symbolic representations of adulthood that attract them. Satanism provides a set of beliefs to meet this need. When combined with its ritualistic mysticism and practices, it is accepted in the mind of many young people as an attractive rite of passage.

Furthering the attractiveness of Satanic cult ritual is the fact that it provides an anchor in times of change. We need to remember that all people tend to look for psychological anchors during such times. Young people making the transition from childhood to adolescence experience a period of rapid change in their lives. The uncertainty that accompanies change, especially at the pace experienced by an adolescent, is good cause for anxiety in most people. In much the same manner that a figure skater focuses on a single object to avoid becoming dizzy, the adolescent is just as likely to lock on to a ritual to cope with the dizzying changes that occur during adolescence. In fact, the greater the rate of change, the less prudent one will be in choosing a supporting ritual. Because of this need, we can predict with accuracy that adolescents who are most vulnerable to Satanism may really be experiencing difficulty coping with the changes occurring in their personal lives.

When blinded by rapid change and resulting feelings of loss of control over their environment, it is easy for the adolescent to grasp at any promise of power and control. Satanism provides the power of freedom by offering adolescents a substitute for the previous attachments to their parents, family, church, school, or any other authority figures who might be found in their personal lives. In fact, those people most vigorously rejected by the adolescent who has found Satanism are those who were the strongest emotional anchors in their lives before their Satanic involvement.

The need for emancipation is well met by Satanic cult systems. However, the entry into the adult world, a second aspect of ritual, is conspicuously absent in the practice of Satanism. Consequently, from a psychological point of view, this is the most dangerous element in the entire problem of Satanism. The task of accepting the responsibilities of adulthood and formal entry into that society is of no concern whatsoever to Satanic philosophy or its related rituals.

Adolescents are further encouraged to focus on the ritualistic nature of emancipation by contemporary social influences that erode a sense of future. The advertising industry, for example, does little to remind us that the future is simply a matter of time. The message of "Buy now, pay later" hammers away at the consumer. The illusion of having everything we want in the immediate present is further promoted by the credit card business. Rarely does a week go by, for example, without most of us receiving yet another application for a credit card, each company locked in intense competition with the others to persuade us to think about buying now, and only in fine print giving any notice of the costly terms of paying later.

In the world of the adolescent nothing is more powerful than the attraction of an automobile. Many young people grow up for a car and in a car. As a result, a great number of young people sacrifice their futures by dropping out of school or school activities to work. They work to buy and support a car. They must have a car to get to work.

The music industry is no amateur in leading young listeners to forget the future. The lyrics of a great deal of popular music promote such narcissistic thought and self-absorption that the future may appear to be as distant as another galaxy to the children and young adolescents who listen to it for endless hours.

Many young people are also led to believe that the inevitability of war is sufficient reason to ignore the future. "What's the use?" many say. "The world is going up in smoke anyway." This pessimistic view of things is a common concern to many adolescents who conclude that the search for world peace is futile. They interpret any thawing of the cold war as simply a shift of concern from Eastern Europe to dangers of Third World countries who have great tolerance for terrorism as a way of life.

The pace of education is also of little consolation to today's adolescent. The demands of contemporary education are of greater magnitude than those of past generations. The greater complexity of academic demands is further complicated by the fact that young people are still confronted with the perpetual demands of adolescence and its psychological developmental processes. Either task, school or coping with adolescence, is difficult enough by itself.

Some young people today are learning in high school what the previous generation learned in college, if the scientific and technical knowledge even existed at the time. The explosive growth of knowledge itself is a major source of frustration. Resigned to defeatist attitudes, some young people never even acquire the knowledge needed for survival itself. Drury (1989) argues that science reduces the image of mankind, stripping away the mystic. Renewed interest in occult beliefs indicates a search for those mystic properties suppressed by science.

Feelings of estrangement, alienation, and the abandonment of a future time perspective are the basic parameters of current reality for many young people. These defenses channeled into the occult world simply shield the troubled young person from the real world challenges of responsible adulthood.

There are even approaches to psychotherapy that would have us believe that the here and now is the only temporal context in which any of us can experience our existence. Many adolescents are fed doses of therapy that nurture only the expression of and sensitivity to current feelings (which is not all bad), leaving little or no attention to the fact that each of us is inexorably locked into an ongoing confrontation with the future. Patterson, for example, captures the contemporary essence of Gestalt therapy: " 'Now' is the zero point between the past and the future, neither of which exists: Only the now exists" (1986, p. 358).

What to do after getting in touch with yourself in the present represents the most difficult stage of effective and professionally conducted psychotherapy. Getting in touch for the moment is a matter of stripping away defenses, a time for reintegration of a worldview. It is the sustaining perspective of the past and the future that provides the present with substance, meaning, and hope. Just as taking apart an engine may be necessary to repair it, the real skill is found in those who can put the engine back together, making it run better than before. So, too, is it a real skill of the therapist to reconstruct a more serviceable view of the world when a previous one falls apart.

Our contemporary society continues promoting the demise of structure and its concomitant rituals that serve to clarify an adolescent's sense of identity. Family rituals, going to church, Sunday dinners, and holiday gatherings, for example, are virtually nonexistent for many adolescents who experience emotional turmoil in their lives. As a result, these adolescents do not have the help to go beyond their narcissistic entanglements and to perceptively see that one's existence is far more meaningful when considered from a broader context of time and space.

Rites of passage should involve commitment. The act of getting away from something implies a movement toward something as well. This is the dual nature of the emancipation issue confronting all adolescents. As a result, adolescents who struggle to free themselves from former patterns of dependency really have two tasks to accomplish. Satanism promotes only the emancipation, but it does so with deadly efficiency.

TOWARD A SOLUTION

The solution to this ritualistic dilemma for our contemporary adolescent is the responsibility of many areas of society. The future should be given greater consideration in advertising, entertainment, education, and therapy. We must balance the significance of "the now" with "the then." It is not until we are able to institutionalize a confrontation with the future through the media and academic intervention that adolescents in the midst of turmoil will see future time perspective as meaningful to their reality.

Second, our society must provide positive rites of passage. Myerhoff (1982) makes good sense recommending that we create our own rituals when the culture fails to do so. However, this advice must be taken only if the rituals support emotional well-being and responsible adulthood. Unfortunately, street gangs have assumed a major role in providing rites of passage for some adolescents in society. When gang members become emancipated from their parents, their acceptance of an adult culture is exceedingly different from and clearly in opposition to the values of contemporary society. This can only be prevented by parents assuming responsibility for providing family rituals that give an assurance to young people that the family is the source of security in their lives. These can include meals together, celebrating accomplishments together, going to church or temple together, or simply being together at certain times every day.

The third challenge we face involves the training of people who enter the helping professions. We can no longer support the illusion that simply "feeling good" for the moment is therapeutic. The proliferation of therapeutic approaches that focus on current affect and emotions must extend themselves into a broader time perspective. It is of little value to free a client, especially an adolescent, from the grip of an emotional problem by simply providing a greater sensitivity to and awareness of the present. We can no longer ignore the fact that dealing with the present to the exclusion of one's past and future simply promotes existential anxiety. As a result, what people may see as good therapy will simply leave many of our teenagers feeling anxious, disenchanted, and unable to anchor themselves into a broader commitment to our society.

Finally, we must address the increasing problem of narcissism that has adversely affected our adolescent culture. Advertising and entertainment continue to promote an attitude that is inordinately concerned with oneself to the exclusion of others. There are few experiences more therapeutic than that of becoming engaged in an activity that takes an adolescent beyond the self. For example, the evidence of an increase in volunteerism is a promising indicator. Our problems are more difficult to address if we do not have the experience of helping others. Within the experience of altruism the impact of narcissism diminishes and the young person is more properly prepared to make an effective and substantive commitment to the greater society.

Satanism gains a firm hold in the mind of an adolescent by meeting the need for ritual and emancipation and by providing an eloquent rationalization for the rejection of adult values. Consequently, it is a half-ritual, effectively facilitating a need for liberation but ignoring the greater need for addressing the future. In short, Satanism provides for a need that our culture has failed to meet.

8

Parent Styles: The Beginning

Adolescents travel a long road to Satanic involvement, and that journey starts in early childhood. Some people believe that otherwise healthy and well-adjusted adolescents can be lured into the trap of Satanic belief systems by a single experience. They confuse the work of Conway and Siegleman (1979) on the involvement with religious cults with the process of Satanic involvement. These writers describe the process of religious cult conversion as a rapid process, one that can be effectively accomplished in a weekend marathon session.

This myth has little, if any, basis in fact. Nearly every case of Satanic involvement that has been portrayed in the literature has shown that the young person had a long history of serious emotional problems that preceded any Satanic involvement. A number of examples of these histories is provided by Carlson and Larue (1989).

The ways parents relate to their small children can later have a significant effect on their vulnerability to Satanism when they become adolescents. Since this early relationship forms the basis of evaluating all relationships, it warrants closer attention.

A look at the childhood experiences of adolescent Satanists can be very revealing. What is often found is a style of parenting that has adversely affected a young person's ability to endure harmful influences, especially as they relate to coping with emotional stress.

Parents of most young people attracted to Satanism are well intended.

Occasionally parents will be involved in Satanic activities with their adolescents; this is a relatively rare occurrence and is not the focus of this book. This chapter focuses on the behavior of parents who object to Satanism, yet act in ways that allow it to flourish within their families. We are concerned only with parents who say they oppose these practices yet implicitly enable them by their behavior.

Parents in these enabling families often share common behaviors. These behaviors do not directly "cause" Satanism to happen in a family, but allow it to fester. Parents who object to Satanism have a responsibility to better structure the environment of their children to ensure that these problems are not inadvertently nourished by a parental lack of attention to the problem.

There are six major ways that parents contribute to the increased emotional vulnerability of their children and influence an individual's decision to embrace the ideas of Satanism. This chapter will evaluate dimensions of parenting that can either weaken or strengthen the adolescent's resolve to avoid the influences of Satanism.

PARALLEL LIFESTYLES

In at-risk families that are predisposed to a variety of problems, parents develop a lifestyle parallel to that of their children. They are concerned with their own interests and activities, which have no relationship to their children's academic or social pursuits. These family members simply have nothing in common. Their family arrangements resemble an apartment complex where residents come and go, barely recognizing or acknowledging the other residents.

The sad consequence of parallel lifestyles is children who are left to define and focus their pattern of interests without the guidance or supervision of an interested parent. The fact that these parents do not find or make the time to share interests and activities is the major reason some young people in these families become so involved in Satanism before the parents have any clue about what is happening.

Young people who are drawn into early stages of Satanic cult involvement will nearly always show signs of that destructive process. Satanic involvement is so blatant in the life of an adolescent that parents cannot be oblivious to it except when they are fully preoccupied with their own problems. Sometimes parents are present, but they are ignorant of the destructive patterns of cult behavior because they are out of touch with elements of normal child and adolescent behavior.

PARENTAL DISTORTIONS

The second characteristic involves the parental loss of a frame of reference from which to see problems properly. They have drifted from the company of other parents who are in similar circumstances. As a result, when their children display unusual or otherwise aberrant behavior, they have no relevant context or frame of reference to evaluate whether this activity is problematic to the normal development of children.

A common reaction of some parents confronted with signs of Satanism in their children is to say, "Sure, I saw that stuff, but it didn't seem like any big deal." They continue, "After all, my son said it wasn't anything serious. He was just fooling around." This loss of context caused by isolation from other parents places the parent in a vulnerable situation. Young people are likely to use this isolation to their benefit in developing patterns of deception in accounting for their behavior.

MEETING THE WRONG NEEDS

A related consequence of a parent's lack of awareness is the practice of dealing only superficially with emotional problems. These parents commonly confuse emotional needs with physical needs. For example, a young child looking for attention may easily be bought off by the parent who thinks that the provision of material things is all that is necessary in being a good parent. As a result, there is an overabundance of material goods in the lives of these adolescents and a corresponding lack of time and effort directed toward meeting their emotional needs.

DENIAL OF PROBLEMS

Because these parents are usually busy and often preoccupied with their own problems, they are also likely to deny family problems when they occur. Investing themselves heavily in their professions, they are loath to admit they are having difficulty raising their children. As a result, they often deny the obvious when it presents itself.

Suggesting to such parents that their children may be involved in Satanism often has a twofold negative impact. First, the cognitive dissonance of such a revelation is likely to generate a good deal of anxiety on the part of the parent. The shock of this news often leads to an intense need to get away from this information. The most effective means of doing so psychologically is to deny that the problem exists.

Second, some parents do not draw a clear distinction between their success at parenting and their personal feelings of adequacy in general. As a result, any news of a child being involved in Satanic activity provokes a very personal and threatened response. The acknowledgment of this involvement would be tantamount to conceding that the parent himself or herself is personally inadequate as a person as well as a parent. This is likely to result in a blanket denial of any information about Satanic involvement.

Parental denial raises some difficult issues for teachers, counselors, or police officers who need to disclose information to parents, especially when the parent is being informed for the first time. This must be done carefully and at a pace that does not provoke a defensive response of denial. In effect, spoon feeding defensive parents with information they dislike but need to know is an effective strategy. In some cases it helps to introduce the topic from a third-person perspective. If parents can accept that some adolescents have problems like this, and see that these problems have origins that make sense, they will be more prepared to accept the idea that this problem might exist in their own families.

RIGHTS PRECEDING RESPONSIBILITIES

Parents are likely to express their defensiveness in subtle ways. One common posture is to place the burden of proof onto the teacher, counselor, or other helping professional who believes it necessary to discuss an adolescent's Satanic involvement. Parents who take this position often find themselves unwittingly defending the behavior of the adolescent who, it turn, takes this defense as tacit approval to continue the activity. In effect, the young person may be dabbling in Satanic practices while the parent is defending the young person's right to free expression and demanding hard evidence of involvement.

The shift in focus from responsibilities to rights teaches many young people a destructive lesson in the process. They are led by parents to believe that responsibilities are secondary to rights. They fail to see that rights are only the logical consequence of responsible behavior.

PARENTAL EMOTIONAL ISSUES

Finally, parents often do not successfully deal with their own emotional baggage. They spend time wallowing in their own problems but have little idea how to solve them. It is no surprise to see their children following the same road to pathology, learning to distort, deny, or, at best, put up with their problems. This mirroring pattern of mutual denial and lack of insight makes intervention difficult, since the parent and the young person are operating their defensive patterns in a mutually reinforcing manner.

An additional problem is created by some parents when they present a set of morals and ethics to their children that is primarily situational in nature. For example, they may object strenuously to any hint of dishonesty from their children, yet see cheating on taxes as an accomplishment worthy of bragging about. Parents who forbid drug and alcohol use by their children may be abusers themselves. They justify nearly every choice, eliminating any absolute right and wrong from the decision-making process. Young people observe their parents unwilling to stand for anything and comfortable shifting their priorities to suit their own needs. Their children read this as hypocritical.

When a combination of negative characteristics in parenting styles exists over many years, adolescents are vulnerable to Satanic cult activity because it provides a great release from the stress, tension, and conflict that come from such parenting.

SOME SOLUTIONS

There is no better protection a young person can have against the influence of Satanism than a long relationship with a parent who is strong, fair, and consistent. There are elements of parenting that provide a sound psychological base for the developing child, elements that foster the ability to cope with temptations involving cults, Satanic or otherwise.

Independence Training

Many parents find it difficult to accept this basic rule of good parenting and discipline: when a child is punished for doing something wrong, it is important that he or she be returned to the same situation to prove that a lesson has been learned by the punishment. For example, a child who is punished for throwing sand in the sandbox needs to be allowed to return to the sandbox to see if the punishment has worked. The adolescent who comes home drunk with the family car needs to be given the family car again to see if his or her punishment for that behavior has had the expected effect on future behavior.

Children need to take on minor responsibilities in order for them to learn to feel that they are in control of their world. As a result, independence training should start as early as a youngster is able to communicate with a parent. Beginning with the most basic tasks such as picking up one's toys or helping with the laundry by matching socks, children can benefit from being expected to help shoulder responsibilities. He or she becomes an important contributing member of the family.

We are often led to believe that a youngster who is well behaved and compliant is a healthy child. This is not necessarily true. In fact, the opposite may be the case. Youngsters who are especially quiet or compliant are learning to be dependent on parents for their self-esteem rather than learning to feel good about themselves by doing something useful. Children must learn to be independent by accomplishing through their own behavior. Many parents find this difficult to accept because a compliant child flatters their ego. These parents erroneously believe that a child who is quiet and does not impose on them is evidence that they are good parents.

An important study by White (1985) has led to conclusions that are of great help to parents in understanding this issue. White and his associates found that youngsters who were independent individuals as well as good leaders were quite different from children who were dependent and passive. These differences were observed in his study among children as young as eighteen months of age. He found a distinct difference between the parents of the two groups.

Children inclined to show leadership ability and independence were raised in homes where parents gave them full access to the house. On the other hand, very young children contained in a restricted environment such as a playpen or crib for safety did not learn to explore their world and achieve the early learning so essential to healthy childhood. They did not learn to control or master their environment.

The second finding made by White and his associates was that the parents of the competent children were good at "kid-proofing" their homes. While they were willing to allow their children full access to the house, they were also very careful to ensure that things that might be harmful were kept well out of their reach.

Another significant finding of this study was that those children who were effective leaders were allowed to work on their own for long periods of time. In fact, parents only intervened to help when the child made a request for assistance. Consistent response to a child in this manner results in the young person feeling a sense of control over the parent. Although this may be unsettling to the parent, it is clear that a child must learn a feeling of control over his or her environment, and the parent is an integral part of that environment.

Another finding of White's study relates to the language used by parents of the competent young children. Their language was distinctly different in two regards. First, they spoke to their children more frequently, and their children were exposed to much more live language than were the less competent children. These parents took the time to talk to their children on a one-to-one basis rather than allowing them to acquire language from the radio or television. It appears that some parents believe that a child will learn language just as well by sitting in front of a television. However, since the child has no obligation to interact with or respond to that television, he or she is much less successful in the development of good language skills. Secondly, the parents of these more capable children were also careful to use correct grammar, pronunciation, and sentence structure when talking to their children.

Finally, White concluded that the parents of more effective children were also very good disciplinarians. They not only responded with appropriate discipline whenever the child misbehaved, but they also responded with a good degree of affection whenever the child properly deserved it. When raised in this type of environment, the child quickly learns that he or she can obtain all the affection and praise that is desired. All the youngster needs to do is behave in an appropriate manner.

An implication of this finding is the destructive potential of inconsistent parents. A hallmark of seriously disturbed adolescents is the family background characterized by inconsistent parent responses that were commonly abusive and violent (Haizlip, Corder, & Ball, 1984). It is essential that parents not allow their own mood states to overshadow their responsibilities for dealing with their children appropriately. Praise and affection should be given consistently by parents in response to appropriate behavior.

One of the common problems with young people who become involved in Satanism is that they are driven by a need to obtain acceptance and affirmation and are usually unable to obtain this at home. As a result, they look elsewhere. It is clear that many cult members are extremely effective at praising, affirming, and bestowing affection on young people who express interest in their activity. A major technique of induction into many religious cults is known as "love bombing" (Galanter, 1989). Satanic cult recruiters demonstrate a perverse form of this process of "love bombing" by heaping approval on actions that were previously thought to be wrong or immoral.

Limit Setting

One of the most common difficulties reported by parents in raising children involves the setting of appropriate limits. Often, parents whose youngsters get into trouble during adolescence have raised their children in homes where limits are either too tight and restrictive or too loose and poorly defined. This becomes a problem during early adolescence when teenagers are likely at some time to test limits that are imposed on them.

It is especially important for parents to remember that limits are an essential part of the parenting responsibility and they must be maintained at all times, especially during adolescent rebellion. The ritualistic nature of Satanic cult activity is very precise in setting limits. As a result, it is likely that adolescents who are unable to obtain limits from their parents may often find them in their participation in this cult activity.

Parents often fail to recognize a child's testing and pushing of limits as an attempt to determine how much hassle a parent is willing to go through for them. It becomes a measure of how much a parent seriously cares. Finally, it is important to keep in mind that a prerequisite to mature adulthood is the internalization of limits, that is, the ability to set limits for oneself without input from another person. The way in which adults gain the ability to set limits is often determined by the extent to which their parents were willing to impose these limits externally on them as children. Eventually limits become part of an individual's personal value system and are an expression of their attitudes about what will constitute appropriate behavior.

Limits that are too strict and that are enforced in a heavy-handed manner are also a concern to therapists working with those who are involved in cult activity. For some adolescents cults justify the opposition to structure imposed by well-intended parents. Young people limited in a restrictive, unfair, or occasionally brutal way will seek ways to avoid that response in the future. Children and adolescents need the opportunity to test limits and engage in common adolescent rebellion.

During this time they often will assume attitudes and values that contradict those of their parents. In the vast majority of cases adolescents will outgrow this period of rebellion and assume a position of responsible adulthood in the community. During this time of rebellion and acting out toward values contrary to those of their parents, adolescents need to experience their parents' commitment to these values and seriousness about enforcing them. In addition, they need to know that limits may be flexible on occasion, but that they never break. For example, a curfew rule should be set for an adolescent, but exceptions may occur that warrant a flexible interpretation of the rule. Nevertheless, a curfew always exists.

There are some general rules of thumb that parents should keep in mind when setting limits in dealing with their children. First, it is important that the limit or consequence provided by a parent is something over which the parent has control and that he or she is willing to enforce. For example, a frustrated parent who grounds a child for misbehavior for "the rest of your life" is imposing a greater punishment on himself or herself than on the child. The consequences for exceeding limits should be enforceable and fair and should occur within a reasonable time period.

Young people will test limits to determine how seriously parents care about them. This type of limit testing is often a backhanded way of asking for attention, affection, or some other expression of concern. A sensitive parent can reduce this need considerably by providing responses of concern and affection rather than engaging in a power struggle. For example, hugging a frustrated teenager trying to argue with you is more productive than engaging in the argument. I have listened to a significant number of adolescents complain that parents simply do not care about them enough to punish them when they do something wrong. This indicates that one's need for affection may very well be an underlying motivation on the part of a young person who engages in limit-testing behavior with his or her parent.

Finally, it is important for parents who engage in good limit setting to remember that objective limits will work better than those which are subjectively determined. An effective way to state a limit is to put it in writing and to post it on the door of the refrigerator. This serves three purposes. First, the limits are farther removed from the relationship between the parent and the child. Second, the parent is able to impose a limit and simultaneously have compassionate concern for what imposition that limit has on the life of the youngster. Another advantage is found in the fact that most children and adolescents go to a refrigerator so often that they probably will be very familiar with these limits.

Double Binds

The most harmful error of ineffective parenting, one that can lead to a variety of emotional problems, involves the imposition of double-bind situations on a frustrated child. A double bind is a situation in which a youngster finds himself or herself caught, with no way out. For example, a mother is extremely frustrated with her child who is in the middle of a temper tantrum. This frustration is greatly increased by the fact that the mother is in the grocery aisle at a local food store. Her only response to the child, who by now is screaming and out of control, is "Shut up, or I'll spank you." This is a classic case of double bind. The child is so emotional that he has no capacity to quickly gain control of himself in the short period of time ordered by the angry mother. This child has no way out. He is out of control and he is going to get smacked because his mother is also out of control. Double binds convince the child that he or she has no ability to affect his or her world. They violate a fundamental concept of child development that obligates parents to remember that their youngsters must learn to control their environment.

Double-bind situations also are common sources of guilt feelings for a young child. For example, some parents will angrily pick up a child when he or she is pleading for attention or affection. Grabbing a pleading and pestering baby in an angry or hostile tone of voice will put a child in a very subtle but powerful double bind. He or she has a strong need for attention and affection at the time of this pleading but he or she must also experience the anger of the parent in order to get some degree of attention to meet the basic need expressed. This young person must pay the price of a significant amount of guilt in order to get the attention he or she desires from a parent. Young people who find their way into cults, especially Satanic cults, appear to have common problems of guilt from which the ritual of a cult provides an escape.

In some cases guilt feelings come from styles of parenting that have occurred over years of growth and development. In many cases feelings of intense guilt can be traced to subtle cases of double binds that occur during childhood.

In summary, repeated exposure to double-bind situations can be damaging to a young child. A basic building block for a sense of control over one's life as well as a major attribute of developing a sense of integrity involves the ability to control the environment and properly deal with guilt feelings. A parent who shows great concern for the mental health of his or her child will recognize that children must be able to make decisions that enable them to exert control over the environment.

Praise

Many parents believe that praising children as much as they can is an effective way of building self-esteem. This is true, but only partly so.

Praise without good cause, given to a child who does nothing but simply exist, is likely to encourage the child to pursue manipulative means of obtaining praise later in life. On the other hand, a child who learns early in life that praise is rewarding and satisfying and can be obtained by doing specific things will learn better control over how it is obtained. This use of praise is another example of how a child might learn to feel a degree of control over the parent.

If a child learns early that praise can be obtained by simply doing something constructive, he or she learns to control the parent as one who gives praise, and consequently, controls the behavior used to obtain praise. This is different from a child who learns to obtain praise by being cute, being quiet, or somehow being manipulative. While love is unconditional and not dependent upon a child's performance, praise should accompany a child's efforts to accomplish certain tasks or goals and not result as a mere consequence of being.

Another problem with the use of praise is that it is often contingent upon the mood of the parent. In many cases a youngster will misbehave repeatedly and the parent will respond with an honest attempt to correct the behavior. It often occurs that when the youngster finally behaves appropriately, the parent is so frustrated by that time that he or she responds by ignoring the child rather than by giving praise. What a young person learns in this situation is that if you want attention, misbehave; if you want to be ignored, behave yourself. Almost every youngster will opt for obtaining attention rather than being ignored.

Redirecting Inappropriate Behavior

A concept known as "reciprocal inhibition" was introduced by Wolpe (1958). Basically, Wolpe argued that one cannot experience two contradictory feelings at the same time. We use this principle in our everyday coping with the world. For example, if an environment makes you frightened, you will try to make light of the situation to ward off feelings of fear. Laughing off a close call in traffic reduces tension and dissipates the fear that would ordinarily come from a near-accident.

This coping is also seen in young people who, for example, will impulsively engage in laughter and childish giggling when they are placed in tense or apprehension-producing situations, such as a wake or funeral. The impulsive humor allows a youngster to avoid feeling anxious or apprehensive in that tense and unfamiliar environment. The concept of reciprocal inhibition also applies to parents' management of their emotions. Parents have been heard to say they don't care, for example, when they care very much about their children.

Young children are notorious for engaging in a period of crabby, obnoxious behavior before going to sleep at night. Many parents are probably inclined to believe that babies are engaged in a conspiracy to make parents crazy. Although it may seem this way, this is not true. These young children must find an opportunity to vent the frustration and tension that has built up during the day. What they are attempting to accomplish is catharsis, that is, an unloading of their emotions. This is not different from what we do in adult life. Many people report that crying provides them a significant release of tension and enables them to feel more calm. In fact, most people will agree that crying is a therapeutic experience. Young children behave in exactly the same manner. Their need to release tension is simply more frequent than that of most adults, and their choice of style for the release of tension is age appropriate.

As young children get older and engage in developing defense mechanisms to shield themselves from emotions, they often find themselves in the position of feeling tense or anxious but having no understanding as to why they feel that way. In these cases they need to express a basic emotion to regain better control of themselves after the frustration of the day.

A perceptive parent can help a young child by providing positive opportunities for emotional expression. In the case of a fight or argument, the child will obtain a release of tension and frustration but he or she will also carry away from that experience feelings of guilt and resentment that have consequences of their own. The guilt may lead to negative behavior or resentment toward the parent and will enable the young person to rationalize rejecting the parent as well as their values. These feelings of resentment and guilt experienced together are effectively resolved by engaging in ritualistic behavior that characterizes Satanism.

Responding to Feeling

A parent who is alert to the emotional needs of the child can usually detect a difference between what a child is saying and the intensity of emotion that goes along with that statement. Usually children in these circumstances will say things with a level of emotion out of proportion to what is being said. For example, a parent who asks a child to pick up her coat may get an angry response like, "Why are you always nagging me?"

The parent may take one of two options. He or she may engage in a debate with the child about why he or she is not always picking on the child, which results in a negative and tense encounter leaving both parent and child frustrated and bewildered. In this case they both leave that conversation with stronger feelings of resentment and become set up for more communication problems around other issues.

A second option available to a parent in this circumstance is to respond to the feeling and ignore the content of the statement. For example, a parent who gets a response about nagging might simply say, "You are really angry about something. How come?" This type of response will serve two purposes: First, it tells the child the parent is aware that something is out of step. Second, the "How come?" gives the child the opportunity to explain that something else is going on. Although a youngster may not respond to this parental invitation, it will tell the child that the parent is not going to be hooked by the response. This message communicates a level of emotional understanding that goes beyond the awareness of the child. As a result, this response will assist a young person to become more sensitive and aware of emotions as they occur.

Self-Disclosure

Many parents engage in long monologues about their own childhood whenever they are asked for advice from a child. There are five deadly words in being a good disciplinarian. These are "When I was your age."

There are three reasons why parental self-disclosure becomes a problem for a child. First, as adults, our recollection of childhood and adolescent experiences is not as accurate as we would like to believe. We tend to forget unpleasant experiences that are common to this age of development. Also, we tend to make things up to fill in blanks in our memories with things that never happened quite the way we recall them. In fact, this process is well known to lawyers who find that witness testimony is not as accurate as the witness would like to believe. They have given a term, *confabulation,* to this process of filling in the blanks.

For example, a father attempting to console his nervous daughter on her first date may use a "when I was your age" style of monologue. There is no question that most parents would love to forget their first date, and usually have, in fact, forgotten that they were awkward, embarrassed, insecure, and convinced that they were as clumsy and awkward as they felt. The impact of this confabulation on the teenager preparing for a first date is that the parent conveys a lack of understanding of the emotions of that experience.

The second problem in our use of self-disclosure is that life for today's adolescent is different from life when we were children. They are exposed to many life situations that never occurred in our lives as adolescents.

A third problem associated with parental use of self-disclosure is that it takes the focus off the person who is experiencing a problem. Some adolescents report that parents have such a strong need to talk about themselves that they show no interest in hearing about the problems of the teenager. When a parent communicates disinterest, a young person looks elsewhere to be understood. An important draw for cults is their proficiency at conveying feelings of understanding to people who do not feel understood by their families.

A general rule about self-disclosure can be made. First, if you can disclose feelings that you experienced in a particular time, it is appropriate. For example, a self-disclosing comment to an adolescent on her first date about your feelings of fear and anxiousness can be consoling. A child can then see that those feelings are not as overwhelming as they seem at the time. However, disclosing how a problem was solved is not as effective.

Role Models

Parents play a major part in shaping their children's behavior by being a role model. There is little question that children will pay more attention to what a parent does than to what a parent says. As a result, parents must remember that effective role models are people who have principles and are willing to stand for something. Many parents find it difficult to state with conviction the values and attitudes that they want their children to hold and incorporate into their own lives. Some parents make the mistake of trying to befriend children rather than dealing with the responsibilities of being a role model.

In many cases parents are not aware that their behavior serves as a model for youngsters nor do they know who is observing their behavior. Parents must confront the unpleasant reality that they are almost always "on display."

Young people who become involved in Satanism may express bitter feelings toward parents because they sense hypocrisy in the parents' system of values and attitudes. These feelings of resentment often focus on issues relating to religion and morals. As a result, many young people have found a basis for rejecting religion simply because a parent's practice of that religion is hypocritical. These are parents who are often abusive, violent, or otherwise ineffective but who persist in regular church attendance.

Young people exposed to Satanism find that cult activity facilitates the rejection of parents' religious convictions. If they become involved, they will commonly reject the parent, their religion, and any practice of that religion. Few adolescents, especially those in the middle of emotional turmoil, are able to distinguish between the overall value of a religion and the parents' hypocritical practice of that religion.

Punishment

The number of children who are victims of abuse and violence in the home has become dangerously high. It is fundamental to good parenting to be cautious about the use of physical punishment. A preponderance of research on violence in the home has concluded that violence begets violence.

Parents who respond to their children in violent ways are likely to find their children using violence to solve their own problems outside the home. When a young person learns that violence is a viable solution to problems, you can be sure that the next generation of parents will assume their parenting responsibilities with the same propensity for violent behavior.

Many parents use physical punishment to unload personal frustrations and hostilities that are unrelated to the child. In these cases, a young person will recognize that punishment is not a function of his or her behavior but the result of what mood the parent is in at the time. As a result, there are greater feelings of helplessness on the part of a child since he or she is unable to control the mood of the parent. All he or she learns is how to cope with punishment.

In these cases young people will often try to manipulate the mood of the parent in order to avoid being punished. This is a common strategy in homes where domestic violence and abuse is common. The child who feels helpless must resort to manipulative strategies to avoid harm.

What abusive parents have learned is that physical punishment is the most effective way to suppress inappropriate behavior. Whenever a child is doing something wrong and a parent responds with physical abuse, the inappropriate behavior is usually eliminated. In fact, the more intense the punishment, the more effective it is in suppressing behavior. However, punishment typically has some very dangerous side effects.

First, punishment increases a child's dependence on the parent despite the fact that the parent is the one who is administering the punishment. Second, it often increases a young person's distance from the parent, resulting in a desire to leave as soon as possible. As a result, there is often a transfer of dependence from the parent onto some other person or group in order to facilitate this separation from the parent. In the case of Satanic cults, the person to whom this dependence is directed is usually less concerned with the interests of the adolescent and more concerned with the goals and objectives of the cult.

The third consequence of punishment is that it can cause aggression toward others. This is commonly called the "bully" syndrome and may be seen with young children. These young people are aggressive and violent in schools and in the neighborhood because they have learned that aggression and violence is an effective solution to problems in the home.

Finally, the use of punishment will almost always cause strong negative feelings toward the person who is administering the punishment, commonly the parent, an otherwise important source of love and consolation for the child. This places a youngster in a double bind. He or she must see the parent as a caregiver and provider but also as the person who inflicts pain. This double bind can be effectively resolved by participating in Satanic cult activity.

When evaluating the long-term effects of punishment, it is difficult to conclude that it has any practical use in the management of children. Physical punishment has far more problems associated with it than its use warrants.

Parent Problems

Some people who become involved in Satanic activities have left homes where the parents have a significant number of problems of their own. A common practice of emotionally disturbed parents is to unload their problems on their children. In many cases young children who are the object of this communication learn to feel responsible for the emotional problems of the parent. This style of parenting may lead a young person to experience guilt-related problems that have no positive solution.

The only resolution to this dilemma is to withdraw from the parent or to look for ways in which this guilt can be relieved. Cult activity, especially Satanism, is effective because it turns guilt into a positive feeling. The message sent by the Satanist is that guilt is good, and it should be pursued. This reversal of emotional values is an inviting solution for the adolescent who cannot otherwise manage guilt feelings.

Single parents can have difficulty managing their own personal guilt. Many single parents who have custody of their children report that guilt strongly affects the relationship with their children. A child who has the opportunity to play one parent against the other will often try to manipulate the guilt of the custodial parent to exact freedoms and privileges by comparing those circumstances to the treatment the youngster gets with the noncustodial parent. For example, if a child reports that she is not required to wash the dishes with the noncustodial parent, the custodial parent may withdraw from requiring appropriate responsibilities.

SUMMARY

Management of child behavior has enormous implications that extend long into the future. Young people who become enamored with Satanism during their adolescence have been primed for that experience in childhood. Parents concerned about raising their children in a healthy emotional environment should pay careful attention to the ways they enact roles as disciplinarians.

9

Communicating Effectively

Communication in its broadest sense is the influence two people have over each other. While it pervades all human interaction, it is difficult to define and even more troublesome to change. This is especially evident in parent-child relationships.

The quality of communication between parents and their children affects the mental health of both parties. Certain patterns of destructive communication can literally drive a young person crazy. It is no surprise that young people who find Satanism attractive often have suffered from ineffective communication between themselves and their parents. This chapter will discuss five major barriers to effective communication. Communication breaks down quickly in emotionally tense or frustrating situations, and during family crises.

Young people involved in Satanic cults often develop patterns of communication that are difficult to penetrate. They invent private meanings for words, unbeknownst to parents or others who attempt to communicate with them. For example, most Satanic writings reverse the meaning of bad and good. What everyone thinks is bad, the Satanist interprets to be good. Telling these adolescents that Satanism is bad will simply be interpreted as further encouragement to continue Satanic cult activity. How to avoid the communication problems created by these private meanings will be discussed.

WHY COMMUNICATION IS IMPORTANT

The number of young people who feel alienation, detachment, and the inability to make meaningful connections with other people is increasing. These young people drift farther and farther from family influences and eventually wind up in a double bind. They cannot communicate with family members and are vulnerable to external influences that do not serve their best interests.

Feeling understood is powerfully therapeutic. For most of us, talking about problems with others helps to clarify attitudes and beliefs and it puts our feelings in a better perspective. Simply thinking about problems is not sufficient to deal with many of the struggles we encounter. Ongoing and effective communication with another person keeps problems from overwhelming us.

Good communication is especially needed when levels of emotion intensify, as they often do during adolescence. During this time feelings run strong and are often in conflict with the rapid changes that occur in the life of an adolescent. The result is a very confusing experience for many young people. To help adolescents clarify the turmoil that surrounds them, we need to remember three guidelines for effective communication.

First, we should convey empathy. We need to acknowledge that the adolescent's feelings about his or her problems are significant and that they need to be recognized and understood. Second, good communication includes respect for the adolescent, with the message that the adolescent has enough value to hold the attention of the parent. Finally, communication, when effective, conveys a degree of concern for the broader experiential world of the adolescent.

Too often parents minimize the significance of adolescent problems because they are uncomfortable about those issues themselves or would rather forget that those problems existed when they, too, were young. Young people subconsciously interpret this to mean that parents do not understand their problems or simply don't care to hear about them. When this feeling surfaces in the adolescent you can be sure he or she will look to someone else for the empathy, respect, and expressions of concern that lend meaning and significance to their lives. Where they look can be the start of serious problems.

The quality of the relationship between an adolescent and his or her parent can be evaluated by looking at the style of communication that has evolved between them. Communication styles develop over years, and positive communication requires an enormous amount of practice and repetition. The implication is clear; parents should address communication issues starting from childhood to ensure that the lines of communication are open and available during the stormy times in adolescence. Five barriers must be overcome before parents can make sense to their adolescents.

BARRIER I: PARALLEL COMMUNICATION

When a person decides to speak, he believes the other person or persons are listening to what is being said. However, when you observe a group of people engaged in animated conversation, often no one seems to be paying any attention to what the speaker is saying. Rather than listening to the other person, each is waiting for the other to stop talking so he or she can begin. Instead of putting an effort into listening, the second party is thinking about what he or she is going to say as soon as there is some silence. This barrier to communication is known as "parallel communication."

As family members communicate in this fashion over time, there are some potentially unhealthy repercussions. First, conversation between family members becomes increasingly more superficial. These people may talk for hours and never have any substance in their conversations. People who talk for long periods of time while saying very little probably have had a lot of experience communicating in parallel fashion.

Second, in both family and marriage relationships, a common problem that results from parallel communication is that one person will look outside of the family relationship for a sensitive listener. This is the origin of the common line: "My wife doesn't understand me." What this really means in a closer evaluation of marriage problems is that the husband and wife in this situation have nurtured the development of strong patterns of parallel communication.

Teenagers who become hooked into Satanic cults desperately avoid family interactions because they have found more meaningful patterns of communication outside the home. Many cult leaders are often charismatic and influential, so it is no surprise when young people exposed to poor communication at home are attracted to those leaders who convey greater emotional understanding and acceptance.

Many people involved in recruiting Satanic cult members have the initial capacity to relate to others in a sensitive and caring manner that is extremely attractive to adolescents, especially if they are unable to feel those emotions in the home.

BARRIER II: MISSED ATTRIBUTION

The second barrier to effective communication in the home is missing attribution. Missed attribution problems result from developing language patterns that allow family members to avoid responsibility for what they say or do by attributing blame elsewhere. For example, we often hear people say, "Look what you made me do" or "You really make me angry" or, in its most absurd form, "The devil made me do it." This language pattern of misplaced blame is learned behavior. No one acquires this kind of language without having been shown its use. Since it must be taught and repeatedly demonstrated before it can be used effectively, missed attribution is a lesson taught at home.

The second destructive consequence of missed attribution problems is that these statements all communicate a message of helplessness. They foster the belief that someone else is in charge of our feelings, our actions, and our thoughts. If I can persuade myself to believe that someone else is in control of my happiness or my emotional well-being or even my sanity, I have achieved the questionable status of no longer being responsible for myself. There is a persuasive body of research conducted by Seligman (1975) that concludes that feelings of helplessness are related to problems of adult onset depression that occur in many people during the early years of their adult lives.

There are people involved in the world of Satanism and other destructive cults who would be more than happy to assume responsibility for children's feelings, emotional states, and behavior. Nearly all cults will instill the belief that the family is the enemy. Once this step in mind control is accomplished, communication with the family breaks down, and major problems are inevitable.

Parents should take care to prevent learned helplessness. A simple rule is to remind a youngster on as many occasions as possible that the child is, in fact, in control of what he or she says, thinks, and does. Too many people fail to remember that the bottom line for all of us is that we are the only ones who are in control of ourselves. We cannot legitimately give that responsibility away.

BARRIER III: PERSPECTIVES ON FOREVER

The third barrier to effective communication involves the use of "forever statements." These trigger a response that seriously disrupts good communication. For example, an angry parent may say the following to a recalcitrant teenager: "You're always late" or "You're never here on time." Whenever those absolutes, "always" and "never," are used, you can be assured that any response will be negatively affected by perceptual threat, a condition of emotional stress that impairs judgment. Under conditions of perceptual threat, our ability to think and make decisions narrows and becomes more rigid than usual. Although this may sound like a subtle distinction, it has a profound effect on communications.

Consider, for example, the last time you got into an argument on the telephone. If you are like most people, you stumbled through the dispute and, only after hanging up the telephone, thought of many great things you should have said. Unfortunately, these things rarely come to mind while we are on the telephone in the middle of the argument. The reason is simple. Perceptual threat resulting from an argument like this triggers such a rigid and inflexible pattern of thinking that we are left nearly incapable of giving effective responses. As a result, we are unable to use our intelligence normally.

Whenever an adolescent is given an absolute, he or she is likely to search for and respond with an exception. For example, if you were an adolescent and your mother told you that you were *always* late to school, chances are you will respond with a counterexample. You would probably search your memory for a day when you were, in fact, on time to school, if not early, just to prove her wrong. The point is this: whenever threatened by a statement that might make us look foolish or incompetent, our natural tendency is to defend our position, regardless of whether that position should be defended or makes any sense at all. We don't think about it, we just do it.

Especially when dealing with teenagers in frustrating situations, remember that the greater the threat, the more incompetent their behavior. Teenagers, under the right conditions of perceptual threat, will do or say many dumb things. They are not really dumb, but they are simply reacting to a great deal of perceptual threat, and this is often precipitated when "forever statements" are used in conversation.

These messages of perceived threat can also create a common psychological phenomenon affecting youngsters who gravitate to cult activities. When threatened in a heavy-handed manner to behave, young people will often engage in the opposite behavior. In fact, psychologists refer to this tendency as an oppositional behavior disorder in cases where an adolescent's behavior becomes seriously disruptive.

When searching for a counterexample to the command to be good, an adolescent may gravitate to a Satanic cult because it represents the epitome of oppositional behavior. This is not so much the result of Satanic cults having any great attraction: they simply exemplify the opposite of that which is expected of teenagers in many homes.

BARRIER IV: HIDDEN ANXIETIES

Any time you sense that an adolescent's emotional response is out of proportion to a statement or a question, you should suspect that a hidden anxiety is operating. An unwritten rule for most adolescents is that feelings of inadequacy, stupidity, or anxiety may not be expressed or otherwise displayed in the company of peers. Whenever experiences provoke these emotions, normal adolescents will typically hide those feelings and unload them at some later time in a safe environment, usually the home. As a result, the release of many hidden anxieties are aimed at parents in ways that sometimes are baffling. This should not be a great surprise. In fact, it is a backhanded compliment that the teenager has sufficient trust and confidence in parents to unload hidden anxieties at them. Releasing hidden anxieties at home has psychological value. The adolescent has the opportunity to unload feelings that, if left to fester, may lead to impulsive or destructive behavior outside the home.

Any time an adolescent's responses are out of proportion to the situation, the young person should be reminded that there is probably a hidden issue. A simple statement like "You certainly sound angry" may be sufficient as a reminder. At other times, a concerned parent might need to be more assertive: "This is creating too many problems for us. You've just got to tell me what's *really* bothering you." The response must be completely calm and natural. Parents who attempt to overstate their reactions with too much emotion may actually drive their adolescents farther away.

BARRIER V: VAGUE MESSAGES

We cannot communicate needs or expectations to our children unless they are specific and can be monitored. Parents might describe their son or daughter as having an "attitude problem," for example, or they might claim that their child needs to "shape up." When I was a boy, my mother told me to "grow up" whenever I was caught in the act of doing something wrong. Although these statements are well intended and express a desire for change, they are too imprecise to be of practical value to a frustrated and troubled adolescent.

This vague communication leads to the playing of the definition game. When a parent speaks to an adolescent in this vague manner, the angry adolescent will insist that the parent provide a better definition. If you tell your child he or she has an attitude problem, you can be sure he or she will want to know what specifically constitutes an attitude problem. You are left with the task of defining "attitude problem" specifically, and if you are not sure of the desired behavior you are trying to obtain, your good intentions will simply be interpreted as nagging with little positive outcome. The problem you attempted to resolve never is addressed because you are left with the equally frustrating task of trying to define it.

Parents who are imprecise in communicating what is wrong may actually be creating a problem outside of themselves to avoid a problem going on inside themselves. For example, if a parent is bothered by something in his or her own life, it is tempting to create artificial problems externally and complain vigorously about them. For example, parents with serious marriage problems may often focus on the problems of their children in order to avoid confronting their more personal problems. This provides the parent with an opportunity to vent frustration stemming from the real problem, but is an effective way of alienating an adolescent and motivating him or her to look elsewhere for better communication.

COMMUNICATING DURING CRISIS SITUATIONS

Many young people who find themselves drawn to cults have come from family backgrounds that have had their share of emotional crises. These families appear to experience one crisis after another, never quite through muddling their way out of one problem before another descends upon them. However, these crises themselves do not predispose the adolescent to involvement in emotional problems of Satanism, but the way in which they are handled can. Difficult but effective problem-solving in the family is an essential prerequisite for developing coping skills and the mental toughness necessary to be an emotionally competent adult. Most adolescents emerge from family crises with a greater preparedness for responsible adulthood. Others, however, are emotionally scarred and have an impaired ability to discern the falseness of Satanism's promises.

If we contrast families that handle their problems well with those that are torn apart by crisis, seven characteristics emerge that reveal more clearly how and why these families succeed under adversity. If you apply the principles they follow to your family during difficult times, you will help your son or daughter avoid much of the emotional strain that predisposes them to a wide range of problems during adolescence.

Ownership

The first of these principles involves how we deal with a common childhood reaction to a family struggle. When a significant family crisis erupts, younger children often tend to see themselves as responsible for these problems. They assume a measure of ownership that does not rightfully belong to them. The younger the child, the greater this tendency. When parents go through a separation or divorce, for example, a common feeling for young children in the family is responsibility for what happened. It is important for parents to take some time to remind their children that they are not responsible for family crises and should not bear any of the guilt for problems over which they have no control.

Guilt can devastate them. First, their security has already been shaken badly and their capacity for basic trust is considerably eroded. This leaves them feeling partitioned from the rest of the family members, emotionally alone, ignored, and often unwanted. These emotions strike at the child's developing sense of identity. The scars will have a long-standing impact on the child's emotional development. Too often, the implications are not seen until adolescence.

Second, the overwhelming guilt is coupled with an equally devastating sense of helplessness. Self-blame is very difficult for a child to handle alone. When the inability to correct a problem is linked to this guilt, a potentially dangerous situation results. The plight of an adolescent, for example, struggling to hold together a disintegrating family is extremely traumatic.

Adding further to his or her difficulty is the fact that the parents are so often caught up in their own problems that they are generally unavailable emotionally to comfort or support the child. As a result, a youngster attempting to make sense out of these crises becomes increasingly more vulnerable to feelings of self-blame. Without the help of a caring and sensitive parent, the child is left to repress these feelings, pushing them into the subconscious, leaving them to fester until adolescence. At this time coping mechanisms tend to break down, and young people will often engage in reckless and dangerous behaviors to reduce the long-repressed guilt.

Moderate Exposure

Although young children need to know that a problem is occurring in the family, they do not need to be regaled with details. Some parents harm their children by refusing to discuss anything about family problems. Others do just as much damage, and perhaps more, by constantly focusing on these problems with the family. This fixation causes worry and apprehension for the child, who becomes increasingly preoccupied with problems that are essentially not the child's responsibility.

Children need to know that something is wrong when a family crisis occurs, but only to gain an assurance that they are not at fault. Something as simple as "Yes, we do have a problem right now between mom and dad, but it is not your fault and we are working on it." This message places responsibility where it rightfully belongs, assures the youngster that he or she is not a cause of the problem, and conveys hope.

Giving Responsibility

The third principle involves giving responsibility to children when they have a need to be helpful. Parents should allow children to channel their nervous and anxious energies in a helpful manner. This is a productive experience for them at a time when they are having a great deal of difficulty coping. Providing an opportunity for the child to take a constructive role during a family crisis also prepares him or her to better handle problems later in life.

Their need to be helpful could be channeled into any of a variety of activities around the house that might contribute to making things run smoothly. For example, a financial setback may require that a mother return to work. The child who assumes greater responsibility for one family chore, for example, doing the laundry, will feel that he or she is making a significant contribution. When these responsibilities are given in moderation, the resulting feeling of greater empowerment leaves the child with more confidence in his or her ability to handle other problems that may occur.

Role Models

Young children are typically more observant than we might ordinarily believe. For this reason it is a valuable learning experience for the child to observe parents who are consistent in what they say and what they do. Parents who respond to family problems by wallowing in self-pity, or with indecision and helplessness, are teaching dangerous lessons to their children, not to mention ruining their own lives.

It is a basic responsibility of parents to show their children how to solve problems by their own actions. In families where parents are together, seeing both parents work on problem-solving cooperatively is a valuable lesson for the younger child. This lesson will have a great impact in their developing style of managing interpersonal relationships. When they begin to broaden their social circles in late childhood and early adolescence, these skills are of utmost importance to adolescents.

Family Rituals

Teenagers involved in Satanic cults often find their involvement provides a ritualistic means to release anxiety and other pressures that have built up in their lives. If their families have given up their special rituals, Satanism is a substitute for what the family has abandoned. The link between anxiety and rituals should not be underestimated since it plays a major role in the lives of nearly all children and adolescents. While young people are not likely to express their need for rituals directly, it is clear that they tend to cling more tenaciously to rituals in times of strife and turmoil.

We all have a natural tendency to look for psychological anchors during times of change. When family rituals are needed the most, that is, during crisis, they are often ignored. For example, a parent with an alcohol or drug problem may disrupt family dinners, churchgoing, or holiday gatherings, rituals that are a source of great security for a young child. Parents are often unaware of the need for the rituals they have neglected in emotionally difficult times. Problems caused by these disruptions do not usually show up immediately. Parents must be keenly aware of the importance of maintaining family rituals in times of stress.

Quality Time

Too often family problems signal the end of time spent together. The amount of time, energy, and attention consumed by the problems is often the time that parents formerly would have spent with their children. Ignoring the needs of children during crisis weakens any strengths that could be derived from parent-child contact. The simple act of spending time together restores feelings of security and peace of mind not only to the child but also to parents who love their children. Which activities occur between parents and their children is not significant. The simple act of being together is of crucial importance. Spending time together restores perspective on many problems, clarifies priorities, and gives parents, as well as their children, time to see things from a more appropriately balanced point of view.

Humor

When emotional problems take humor out of family interaction, the atmosphere in the home becomes negative. Too much time is spent being angry and depressed. Because of this, we lose sight of the healing power of joy and happiness. When we are out of balance, our families often begin to fall apart because they have failed to maintain good emotional balance in troubled times. The careful process of gently injecting humor into a problem situation does much to restore balance by providing relief from the negative impact of these problems.

These seven principles of communication may be crucial in resolving problems. It is likely that they will be the critical factors that determine whether or not families will be devastated in times of trouble or emerge with a greater sense of emotional well-being and a greater capacity to solve other problems that will come their way in the future.

COMMUNICATING WITH ADOLESCENTS INVOLVED IN SATANISM

When young people become interested in cults, they begin to develop styles of thinking that distinguish them significantly from other adolescents. These differences are especially evident in the ways in which they communicate. Adults attempting to influence the lives of adolescent Satanists will find the following four recommendations helpful to their efforts.

Critical Thinking Skills

A glaring weakness in the thinking of many young people involved in Satanism is in their limited ability to critically evaluate what is true. These adolescents commonly accept anything to be true if it can be found in a book. For example, one book read by many Satanists, called the *Necronomicon,* is accepted as factual by young readers. Three books exposing cult folklore, Carlson and Larue (1989), an encyclopedia of occult folklore by Ashley (1988), and a police-related book by Hicks (1991), conclude that the *Necronomicon* is a hoax written by pranksters who have inadvertently contributed to the contemporary folklore of Satanism.

The popularity of this book illustrates how the critical thinking skills of many adolescent Satanists are unsophisticated. They are often so gullible and naive they will believe anything in print. As long as statements agree with their belief systems and facilitate the expression of anger, they are accepted as true. Estranged young people, desperate for something to believe in, adopt a belief system with no attempt to evaluate the validity of those beliefs.

When people adopt beliefs that have little logical value, anyone intent on providing constructive intervention is normally inclined to challenge these beliefs in a direct and forthright manner. These challenges, however, simply lead a young Satanist to defend the beliefs, thereby encouraging him or her to more fully accept them. Anyone regularly called upon to defend a belief is simply persuading himself or herself to more fully accept those beliefs that are being defended. As parents attempt to dissuade young people from Satanism, they often fail because challenging young people about what they believe encourages them to identify more closely with those beliefs. Rather than asking why a person believes something to be true, it is more effective and persuasive to ask the question, "How have you come to believe this as a truth?" The "why" question provokes a defensive response while the "how" question provokes some introspection.

As we attempt to communicate with young people involved with Satanism, it is important to make this shift from the "what" and "why" questions to the "how" questions for several reasons. First, many young people learn a great deal about Satanism before their parents learn of that involvement. As a result, these adolescents are far more knowledgeable about this information than are their parents, and they are much better prepared to defend these beliefs against challenges from parents who understand little of what they are opposing. This process of challenging adolescent Satanists is more troublesome when adolescents become aware of their parents' ignorance. Many young Satanists interpret their superior knowledge of Satanism as evidence of their power over parents. Some even believe that this advantage over the parent is evidence that Satanism gives power over others, especially those who are authority figures.

A dialogue with a Satanist about how truth is obtained is a more useful communication technique. By focusing on the more general topic of truth you avoid the problem of defensiveness. When young Satanists discover for themselves that they have been uncritical in their own quest for the truth, they are likely to apply this new understanding to their own beliefs.

A second advantage to communicating with Satanists in this manner is the opportunity it provides to discuss related occult ideas and events more objectively. Most Satanists embrace many occult ideas with little skepticism. For example, many believe in telekinesis and werewolves, and they attribute Satanism to the infamous Metamoros murder case. Anything occult, it seems, is fair game for the Satanist to accept without question.

Knowledge as Power

As we discussed earlier, many young Satanists thrive on the ignorance of their parents. They will often attribute their success at hoodwinking parents to the power of Satan at work in their lives. For these reasons it is very important for parents to have some idea about the general beliefs that are associated with Satanism. When parents have some knowledge of the occult, they gain two distinct advantages.

First, if the parent is informed, Satan's supposed "power" has been defeated and rendered useless in conflicts that occur between the parent and adolescent. Second, when a parent acquires a working knowledge of the general aspects of Satanism and no longer has a fear of the unknown, it is likely that meaningful communication between a parent and adolescent can occur on topics related to the occult. Parents who confront the beliefs of Satanism with accurate knowledge and more willingness to communicate are much more likely to have a positive influence when they begin to question ideas about the occult.

Objective Questioning

Many people are understandably uncomfortable when talking to adolescents about Satanic beliefs. As a result, they tend to engage in hurry-up conversations that convey more of an interest in getting done than they do in finding a common ground of mutual understanding.

It is helpful for parents to engage in a pattern of questioning that is not confrontational or hurried. This gives the adolescent an opportunity to reveal weaknesses about Satanic beliefs and provides an opportunity to discuss these ideas. Most youngsters who become involved in Satanism are never given an opportunity to discuss these matters openly. As a result, the information they subsequently believe is biased and inaccurate. Much of this information can be better formulated if a parent engages the adolescent in a style of questioning that is not threatening and that promotes further exploration and disclosure.

An effective strategy for working with people interested in Satanism involves the use of objective and sincere questions. A parent who shows sincere interest in the belief systems of an adolescent is likely to find the adolescent more interested in talking to the parent.

An interested parent should encourage the child to explain his or her beliefs and should take care not to challenge those beliefs until the son or daughter has had full opportunity to explain them. Only after an adolescent has been allowed to fully explain his or her beliefs in considerable detail should the parent reveal his or her own knowledge of Satanism.

A discussion of this type might go something like this: "Why do you think Anton LaVey, being a major proponent of Satanism, would reject the Black Mass, since it is a major expression of Satanic ritual?" (LaVey, 1969, p. 100). This type of question conveys a knowledge of Satanism that is well beyond that which most parents are expected to know. It also conveys a conflict between two systems of Satanic beliefs that many young people do not understand themselves. When a parent is seen as knowledgeable and well-informed, there is no possibility of being hoodwinked by young people who falsely believe they possess supernatural power.

Common Ground

Confrontation with a Satanist about the philosophy of that practice is not a good idea. Such confrontations only further persuade Satanists to embrace their own beliefs. It is simply an exercise in self-persuasion for them. A preferred course of action would be to find an area of mutual interest in the broader domain of mysticism and introduce ideas more compatible with a positive view of life. In this manner a confrontation is replaced by gently nudging the adolescent to look at common ground, therefore diminishing the walls that separate most adolescent Satanists from adults.

I believe that a major attraction to Satanism is in its mystical qualities, ideas that exceed the traditional view of human abilities. In an effort to get to this transcendent level of being, the adolescent Satanist has taken a significant leap of faith to accept most Satanic ideas. The need for a mystical experience is driven by internal feelings of inadequacy, inferiority, and the accompanying anxiety they produce. Consequently, we can better understand the attraction to Satanism as a matter of private internal emotions. This process is explained by Maslow (1969) as a way of locking on to a belief system to avoid anxiety and other emotional problems. In his assessment of the human condition, Fromm (1973) describes four essential human needs: relatedness, transcendence, rootedness, and a reference point for understanding the world. Young people who have failed in these pursuits are alienated, disengaged, and detached from the flow of events in the real world and so they pursue Satanic values.

The mystical attraction of Satanism is understandable when you consider that the influence of mystical and transcendent thought is growing in many areas of human study. We are entering a new age of knowledge that extends the arena of human potential and challenges many assumptions about the limits of the mind. Satanism is predicated on archaic assumptions about the potential of the human spirit. By encouraging young people to explore more current studies of the human mind, we provide a view of the world more rewarding, more positive, and more personally fulfilling than the primitive mysticism claimed by LaVey and other followers of Satan.

The new mysticism in the study of the mind need not be feared. It has evolved beyond the cultic trappings of the recent "new age" movement (Valle, 1989). It needs no guru or cult leader. It is an awakening to the potential inherent in all of us, young and old, and it is a positive alternative to the frustration and disillusionment that motivate some to turn to Satanism.

Scientific studies have found common threads of influence between Eastern mysticism and the practice of psychotherapy (Johanson & Kurtz, 1991). In addition, the body-mind connection in modern medicine is emerging from studies with cancer patients. For example, Siegel (1990) discusses a human capacity for healing that may have a revolutionary impact on the field of medicine. This healing power is recognized by professionals from a variety of disciplines (Carlson & Shield, 1989).

When young people grapple with the normal questions of self-understanding they need tools capable of transcending the moment and providing insight into the power and excitement of self-actualization. It is within a perceptive understanding of ourselves that we obtain a proper understanding of human nature. We should encourage our children to learn more about themselves and to pursue legitimate sources for information about the power of the human mind.

SUMMARY

Ignorance on the part of a parent further empowers a young person already enamored with Satanism. Parents commonly are disturbed by Satanism, claiming that it is too mysterious to understand. This is not true. Satanism is simplistic and contradictory in its assumptions, and it has a great deal in common with the worldly pursuits of debauchery and sexual promiscuity. Parents should not allow a belief system that makes so little sense to intimidate them.

10

Satanism and Suicide

We saw in Chapter 6 that dualities serve a purpose. As opposing concepts, God and Satan serve to define each other. For a teenager who is rebelling and acting out, the parental beliefs and values prescribe the opposing behavior. In both cases each side of the duality clarifies its opposite.

In the duality between life and death, life is given greater meaning by a consideration of death. As a result, many teenagers grappling with the meaning of life will come to a consideration of death, contrasting existence with nonexistence (May, Angel, & Ellenberger, 1958).

For most people an appreciation of life is strengthened by the contemplation of death. Some teenagers, however, caught up in a rebellious need to adopt the opposite of parental values and beliefs, become more preoccupied with death than might be expected. Parents who value life and express that value to their children may find that adolescent oppositional behavior may focus on the antithesis of life values.

Teenagers who act out in ways that oppose parental beliefs and values may find the concepts of Satan and death congruent with this oppositional behavior. Both are in direct opposition to many values of mainstream society. When a young person begins to consider death as something that is fascinating, mysterious, and in some ways appealing, serious problems can develop. Too many teens enamored with death have acted destructively on that consideration.

THE EPIDEMIC OF SUICIDE

The rate of adolescent suicide has increased dramatically in recent years. Maris (1985) reports that the rate of suicide has increased by 287 percent from 1960 to 1980. According to Neiger and Hopkins (1988), suicide is the second leading cause of death among teenagers, exceeded in frequency only by accidental death. Other writers, Allberg and Chu (1990), for example, suggest that suicide is one of the three major causes of death in adolescents, depending on the source of data used. Although the number of young people who take their lives is still fewer than the number in the adult population, adolescent suicide remains a serious problem in our society.

Approximately five thousand teenagers die by their own hand each year. Adding to the complexity and magnitude of this problem is the fact that for every teenager who succeeds in taking his or her own life, there are another hundred or two who attempt to take their lives but survive, for the time being (Neiger and Hopkins, 1988).

The enormous and tragic incidence of suicide indicates that teenagers today are more reckless and less concerned about their safety and welfare than were previous generations. A contributing factor to this problem is the Satanic portrayal of death and the hereafter as glamorous and alluring.

GENERAL FACTORS RELATED TO SUICIDE

In addition to interest in Satanic activity, there are other general factors in our society that predispose a teenager to consider suicide as a solution to problems. A brief review of the major factors follows.

The Complexity of Adolescent Life

Growing up in the 1990s as a teenager is a complicated and difficult task. Teenagers today have many more temptations. For example, the proliferation of drug trafficking on the streets and in schools is an issue constantly facing today's youth. Alcohol abuse, commonly associated with suicide, is rampant (Fowler, Rich, & Young, 1986). Further complicating life is the dramatic rate of change in our world. Futurists conclude that the amount of scientific and technical knowledge doubles approximately every three years (Naisbitt, 1984). Given these conditions, the certainty, predictably, and stability of many aspects of our culture no longer exist.

The Loss of Anchors

Some mental health professionals believe that teenagers who become entangled in Satanism and related problems are raised in families that are more secular than those of teens who are not vulnerable to those influences. The loss or lack of traditional religious or positive spiritual anchors makes individuals more vulnerable to the loss of perspective common to adolescents who commit suicide. With this transience and change that we see in contemporary America, where everything is situational, nothing is for sure. Things once thought to be constant have become variable.

A troubled family that has strong religious values is not without its vulnerabilities, either. A youngster dissatisfied with his or her appeal to God for solutions to daily problems may see the antithesis of God, that is, Satan, as a solution to prayers unanswered. A young person who prays for peace in a troubled family is an example of one who may fall into a complex pattern of vulnerability. Suppose, for example, a child resorts to prayer for a solution to problems of violence in the home. If there is a coincidental subsiding of the violence and the prayers, the child sees these prayers as being answered. If not, that is, the violence continues, what course of action is left for the child? Why does God not listen? Why does this violence continue? The idea may occur to this child that he or she is simply praying to the wrong deity, and that Satan has the answers to these needs.

Parental Unavailability

Because of the number of single working parents today, many teenagers are growing up on their own. Allberg and Chu (1990) cite family problems and communication problems as major factors found among suicidal adolescents. Feelings of alienation from the family are common in this group (Hendlin, 1985). The lack of consistent structure and parental supervision leaves children to construct images of adulthood from their own experience, much of which is significantly affected by the media. Entertainers and music stars bombard the young person with messages of adult behavior that is at odds with the values of most parents.

Altered Time Perspective

Many young people in our society have developed a skewed perspective on time. In the fantasy land of television every problem in life must be solved in sixty minutes, or, if it is a major problem, it may take ninety minutes. Teenagers lose patience and believe that the passage of time is insignificant as a healer. Compressed time perspective affects adults, as well, leaving many parents so preoccupied with their own concerns that they have little time to deal with the concerns of their teenagers.

Busy, successful, and detached parents who are unavailable to their youngsters in times of emotional difficulty are common among teenagers who attempt suicide and who become involved in Satanic cult activities (Bourget, Gagnon, & Bradford, 1988). Furthermore, youngsters involved in cult activities are able to continue their practices because of the lack of interest and involvement on the part of their parents.

Peer Conflicts

Teenagers complicate their lives by creating significant peer pressure or conflicts for each other. Teenagers are remarkably different from adults in their ability to be cruel and inflexible in their evaluations of each other. They can also be much more forgiving than their parents and can quickly reverse their previously held opinions. Many adolescents make major and sweeping decisions about their relationships when they are experiencing this cruelty, before they have experienced the forgiveness and its renewed acceptance. This is why adolescents commonly end a relationship at a time when there is uncontrollable anger. Allberg and Chu (1990) report that peer conflicts and impulsivity are significantly associated with suicidal behavior.

It is important not to dismiss peer pressure situations as insignificant. They play a major role in the lives of teenagers and affect their ability to make decisions because of the psychological process of perceptual threat. Under conditions of emotional stress, we are much less capable of using our senses to their fullest. The greater the unmanageable stress in a given situation, the greater will be the resulting perceptual threat.

The concept of perceptual threat explains much of adolescent behavior and helps us to understand why teenagers do things that most adults think make no sense. Perceptual threat causes people to behave in a rigid, narrow, and often incompetent manner (Combs & Snygg, 1959). Many adolescents rely heavily on peer groups to meet their basic needs for security. Adolescents have increasingly intense feelings about their emerging sexuality, and it is not surprising to find that the use of their sexuality is a powerful tool for obtaining what is believed to be emotional security.

Impulsive Sexuality

Retrospective studies, called psychological autopsies, are evaluations of the lives of youngsters who have committed suicide (Litman & Diller, 1985). These psychological autopsies have found that an extremely high number of female adolescents who commit suicide are sexually active and have fears of being pregnant. Adolescents who find that becoming sexually active is a way to meet security needs also have a price of guilt to pay for this solution. Adolescents who find Satanism attractive are often deeply troubled by feelings of guilt and have a difficult time managing those negative emotions. This combination of factors places adolescents in the classic double-bind situation: in order to meet security needs some adolescents become sexually active; the feeling of security obtained by this sexual activity is often washed out by feelings of guilt that result from compromising a sense of morality.

Feelings of guilt have destructive implications in suicide as well as in Satanic cult involvement. Satanism, in fact, becomes a potential solution for a youngster troubled by concerns over sexuality and feelings of guilt. The Satanic religion, according to LaVey (1969), founder of the Satanic Church, holds that sexual activity is a positive, valuable, and necessary activity for a "healthy Satanist." Since he describes his "religion" as one that holds sexual activity to be positive, he also describes sexual behavior to an immature adolescent in a way that encourages masking any related feelings of guilt.

Although it creates tense and difficult situations for parents, it is important that matters pertaining to the development of a teenager's sexuality be open for discussion. A youngster is less likely to act out impulsively if he or she has an opportunity to discuss these matters in a healthy and appropriate context. Sexual impulsiveness alone is not a valid predictor of Satanic involvement. Young people who become sexually active, however, complicate their lives in ways that lead to potentially serious problems, further disturbing normal developmental sexuality.

In many cases, parents, counselors, and other mental health professionals fail to address issues of sexuality with adolescents, and because of its inherent controversy, it is a taboo subject. As a result, an adolescent who is involved in sexual activity is unable to comfortably discuss its implications with anyone except the peer group. The values surrounding one's sexuality become determined by the peer group and not the parent or other responsible adult. Peer groups that gravitate toward the acceptance of Satanic ideology are highly exploitive sexually.

PSYCHOLOGICAL FACTORS RELATED TO SUICIDE

The predisposition to self-destructive behavior and the vulnerability to Satanic cult activity are found in the psychological development of the adolescent. Anyone attempting to evaluate an adolescent's behaviors should observe those behaviors in terms of their frequency, intensity, and duration. These psychological factors can be found in an individual who is entirely normal and at no risk of either self-destructive or cult-related behavior. As a result, it is important that any emotional problem be evaluated in terms of how frequently it occurs, how intensely it affects the individual, and how long it lasts. Without attention to these criteria for assessment, it is impossible to properly make a perceptive evaluation of an adolescent at risk.

Self-Esteem

Loss of self-esteem is believed by most suicide researchers to be a major factor in suicidal adolescents (Lester, 1988). The easiest way to evaluate an individual's self-esteem is to pay the person a compliment.

In addition, the frequency of negative self-talk is a good indicator. Self-talk involves the internal monologue that goes on in the individual. Often people spend so much time verbally beating up on themselves that they appear worn-out and defeated to everyone without any external justification. If adolescents become proficient enough at negative self-talk, they will be entirely capable of verbally abusing themselves on such a regular basis that an eroded sense of personal degradation will characterize their identity regardless of what is going on externally. The master of negative self-talk persistently takes responsibility for things that go wrong and feels helpless when they work out right.

Learned Helplessness

A troubled adolescent may feel that he or she has no control over certain circumstances. Adolescents beset by relationship problems, for example, often cope by blaming everyone but themselves. As a result, they give themselves an excuse to have the problem, but they have no sense of ownership or responsibility for the problem. Learned helplessness has been the object of a substantial research effort (Seligman, 1975; Abramson, Seligman, & Teasdale, 1978). The adolescent who feels overwhelmed and helpless in spite of obvious options has a potential for self-destructive behavior and is at risk for handing over his or her integrity or responsibility to another person.

The Loss of the Future

For young people at risk for self-destruction and cult-related problems the future has no meaning. Baumeister (1990) contends that the inability to anticipate a happy future leads to the anticipation of no future. For the adolescent whose present moments offer little, the future may seem even more bleak. Society owns a major share of responsibility for the erosion of a meaningful time perspective for young people. The advertising and music industries encourage living for the moment. Satanic cult activity, basically hedonistic in nature, makes sense to a young person who is unwilling to or incapable of looking at the future. LaVey (1969) preaches that religion is for the future and Satanism is for now. Many teens find that suicide is the ultimate expression of no future.

The adolescent who has mastered the skill of negative self-talk can become lured into self-destructive cult activity with or without peer influences. This explains why some young people talk themselves into self-destruction and Satanic cult activities despite warnings about their danger.

The Perception of Loss

Another factor common to suicide is the perception of loss. Kaczmarek and Backlund (1991) report that adolescents are especially vulnerable to loss because they have not fully developed their ego identities. Also, they suggest that their coping skills are not sufficiently developed for this experience in adolescence. In a study of suicidal adolescents, Bar-Joseph and Tzuriel (1990) concluded that ego identity formation at adolescence is an effective buffer against suicidal thinking; that is, most adolescents are too involved with the task of determining who they are to kill themselves.

Hendlin (1985) describes the impact of loss in the life of an adolescent. Whenever we lose something of value, we normally experience transient feelings of depression. This depression often causes a feeling of melancholy or a temporary case of "the blues." Generally, it lasts for a period of time and then lifts, enabling the adolescent to get about the business of his or her life. However, when a feeling of loss strikes an adolescent, it is often accompanied by a considerable degree of anger.

Free-Floating Anger

When an adolescent feels deprived of something of value, he or she is likely to get quite angry. It is in the resolution of the anger that an individual often creates difficult situations predisposing him or her to self-destructive and cult behavior. We saw earlier how the Angry Misfit is drawn to Satanism to justify anger. Similarly, anger has been associated with suicidal ideation in a number of studies (e.g., P. Davis, 1983). The angry adolescent struggles to determine what is of value.

In many cases, teenagers who impulsively pursue quick-fix solutions often generate intense anger because they lack a mature understanding of loss. For example, it is common that the end of an important relationship is associated with a great deal of anger and frustration, which comes from the inability to see beyond that point in time. Suicide nearly always involves the acting out of anger in some form. Less dramatic, but equally insidious, Satanism draws heavily on facilitating the expression of anger, as well. LaVey (1969), for example, exhorts his reader to smash the enemy, in a mocking rejection of the "turn the other cheek Christian."

A teenager who experiences the breakup of an intense romantic relationship may feel extremely deprived and sensitive to the loss. The impact of loss is often underestimated by parents. The parent may feel relief and react to the breakup with a sense of victory, only provoking greater anger on the part of the adolescent. The adolescent may be deeply troubled and see impulsive or dependent solutions as viable during those difficult times. Critical periods of loss are often the result of the ending of a boyfriend or girlfriend relationship that has played a major role in the emotional life of the adolescent (Rotheram-Borus et al., 1990; Strang & Orlofsky, 1990).

The ending of any adolescent relationship should be an indicator to parents and mental health professionals that a difficult time lies ahead for that adolescent. We also must keep in mind that the degree of loss from that ending can only be properly evaluated from the perspective of the adolescent who has experienced the loss. Consequently, this should be talked about, and only in terms of the adolescent's feelings about the loss, not how the parent feels.

RELIGION AND SUICIDE

Adolescents who think about death, suicide, and the occult are often quite introspective and concerned about the meaning of life and death. It is not surprising that many adolescents consider suicide as a result of their thinking about death and its religious and philosophical interpretations. Many people do not make a clear distinction between the death of themselves and the death of another person. Usually, in thinking about death, one views his or her own death from the perspective of another person. What is lacking in the adolescent conception of death is an appropriate appreciation of its finality. So long as death is viewed from this immature point of view, its true devastation and impact are not really understood.

Viewing their own death as the death of another person makes it acceptable, possible, and perhaps even attractive in some cases. Once acceptable, death ceases to have its permanence and becomes a message. We will see that Shneidman (1985) has developed a theory of suicide that is dyadic, that is, involving a message of anger from one person to another.

Some adolescents consider the death of another adolescent as glamorous and attractive. I recall attending the wake of a teenager who committed suicide. The girl in the coffin was described by her friends as looking so peaceful, so rested, and so attractive. These adolescents saw this child in death as being desirable. They were remarking about how beautiful the remains of this young girl looked. Their meaning of grief was belittled by a greater sense of awe. Everything pointed to a denial of the terrible reality that this girl was not asleep, she was dead. The failure to realize the permanence of the child's state, its irreversibility, and its devastating impact on survivors was a serious failure of understanding.

An individual's religious beliefs may also encourage a desirable interpretation of death. The concept of life after death provides the opportunity to view death from the perspective of an observer whose soul continues to live after bodily death. Contemplating the experience of being with God or one's deity is a further enticement to actualize death. Being with a lost friend is also a powerful draw for a teenager if he or she believes there is reunion with the deceased after death.

The typical adolescent has a fascination with activities that lead to death. For example, young people fascinated with military life, weapons, accidents, and funerals have an important psychological reason for their interest. This might be interpreted as a confrontation with death, which for most people is necessary to overcome their fear of it. Adolescents enamored with Satan practice a similar confrontation with death as a way of dealing with their fear of death.

A perceptive parent will recognize the value of contemplating death. This belief has existed for centuries and is found in the writings of many philosophers. Essentially the argument goes like this: our being, that is, our existence, cannot fully be appreciated except in the context of not being (May, Angel, & Ellenberger, 1958). Life is not seen or enjoyed to its fullest until we have experienced or at least contemplated our own death. For an adolescent struggling with the meaning of life, suicide as an alternative to meaninglessness is inviting.

Koestenbaum (1971) writes that the most vitalizing fact of life is the utter inevitability of death. Man is incapable of escaping death. However, the acceptance of death enables one to immediately see the urgency of concentrating on life. If one accepts the fact that death is inevitable, little time should be wasted living a life of fulfillment. Koestenbaum argues that the acceptance of death means simply taking charge of life. As we consider the prospect of our own death, we are obligated to hold a greater value for the meaning of life.

Jung (1959) discusses a long-held religious belief relating to the existence of an Antichrist. To many religious philosophers and theologians, the need for an Antichrist exists in order to provide us with a frame of reference or a background with which to gain a greater appreciation of God. Without an Antichrist, the personification of the opposite of God, we would never reach the full appreciation of the goodness of God.

Taken together, these arguments proposed by Koestenbaum and Jung suggest that just as life and God are necessary elements in the life of an individual, so too are death and Satan. Since they are essential elements in the appreciation of our existence, we need to learn better ways to accept rather than deny them.

THE LINK BETWEEN SATANISM AND SUICIDE: DRUGS

Drugs and alcohol often link Satanic cult involvement and the act of suicide. Some professionals believe that young people may be indoctrinated into Satanic cult activities with a good dose of recreational drugs (Johnston, 1989). These drugs open a young person to some of the more bizarre activities common to a Satanic cult. A study by Fowler, Rich, and Young (1986) concluded that more than half of the people who have committed suicide have also met the criteria for substance abuse. Elsewhere, Rich, Fowler, Young, and Blenbush (1986) concluded that the upsurge of youth suicide is due in part to problems of drug abuse. If half those young people who commit suicide are using drugs, these writers argue that it is reasonable to conclude that suicide is, in some ways, the manifestation of a substance abuse disorder. Drugs may become readily available to a young person when he or she becomes involved in Satanic rituals; access to drugs becomes a benefit to being a Satanist.

Alcohol serves an important role, as well. Anyone toying with the idea of Satanism, but lacking the "courage" to act on the idea, commonly finds himself or herself engaging in that behavior under the influence of alcohol. This happens for two reasons. First, alcohol impairs one's ability to make good decisions. Second, alcohol lowers an individual's inhibitions. Many young people exhibit highly impulsive behavior under the influence of alcohol. A young person contemplating the act of suicide in homage to Satan is likely to acquire some assistance from the heavy use of alcohol in mustering the courage to act on that idea.

Lowered inhibitions, impaired judgment, and self-destructive tendencies often accompany Satanic cult involvement, placing an emotionally unstable adolescent in an extremely dangerous situation.

THE CASE OF RELIGIOUS CULTS

Any discussion of cults and suicide would not be complete without some consideration of the mass suicide and murder that occurred in Jonestown in 1978. Conway and Siegleman (1979) provide a good summary of this catastrophe. In this case a group of religious followers of Rev. Jim Jones moved to Guyana, a small country in South America. There they attempted to build their own city and live in an isolated religious community. One major problem surfaced. The Reverend Jones was not as honorable or emotionally stable as his followers had believed him to be. At a public level, Jim Jones appeared to deny the power and the ego gratification derived from being a religious leader. However, he had a dark side that was not revealed until near the end of his life.

This dark side of Jones showed that his sense of survival was dependent upon his ability to have complete power and domination over his congregation. He isolated himself from authorities who had begun to investigate his group. As a result, Jones's decision to move his congregation to Guyana enabled him to have complete control and authority over his unsuspecting followers. This pattern of control and isolation is a key factor in understanding the mind of a person who becomes involved in cults.

Blos (1962) describes young people who become involved in patterns of delinquency as immature and incapable of coping with normal conflict in their lives, though they are capable of using intelligence and creative abilities. The consequence of this pattern is a failure to recognize and manage dependency needs. These young people find that the cult completely resolves any dependency issues for them when they place their dependency into the hands of the cult leader.

We may argue that this or any other pattern of dependency is unhealthy. However, it leaves an individual with a relatively stable lifestyle so long as the goals and the objectives of the cult are consistent with the interests and well-being of its members. Excessive reliance on any cult to provide protection from problems of emotional dependence can lead to catastrophic consequences, as was the case in Jonestown, where hundreds of innocent people committed suicide at the command of their crazed leader. The point at which this becomes a significant problem is when the individual's sense of identity is no longer in his or her personal control. When young cult members develop a sense of identity that becomes fully dependent upon how the cult leader sees them, they have abandoned personal responsibility, surrendering their decision-making ability to the cult leader. As a result, they become fully dependent on the leader for their mental health, their religious teaching, and their physical survival (Sorrel, 1978). The act of placing this much control in the hands of Jim Jones was a serious mistake.

SUICIDE AND SATAN: THE DOUBLE DRAW

Some investigators of Satanic cults have concluded that cult membership encourages suicide as an act of trust in Satan (Anderson, 1988; Wood, 1987). The argument goes something like this: if you trust Satan enough to take your own life for him, he will reward you for this courageous act by giving you a high position in the Satanic army. This army is supposed to rise up and take over the world at some future time. To most people, this argument would sound like a tale of frightening metaphysical double-talk. However, to a deeply troubled, depressed, and angry adolescent, this message is not as crazy as one might think. A young person who finds his or her life simply intolerable may see this as a good solution. It serves two purposes. First, it takes the individual away from a bad current situation. Second, it holds the promise of a leadership role in the Satanic army.

Ordinarily, suicide attempters report a strong ambivalence and uncertainty about the act of suicide (Shneidman, 1985). They report a sense of intolerable pain in their present lives. They are also much less certain about being dead than they are about not wanting to be alive. As a result, many people contemplating suicide vacillate at great length between the prospect of being dead or alive.

Satanic cults tends to make this position more dangerous for a self-destructive individual. When a person is unsure about being dead, the lack of psychological closure often keeps him or her alive. However, when this uncertainty is replaced with the certain prospect of a leadership role in another life, it no longer serves as a deterrent. The result is dangerous and doubly attractive. The individual is motivated to get away from being alive and is now also drawn to the prospect of being dead rather than being frightened by it.

Parents who see excessive risk-taking or self-destructive behavior in their children should be especially careful that this does not find expression in Satanic cult involvement. One thing parents should look for in the belongings of their youngsters is physical evidence of Satanic cult activity. Nearly all young people involved in Satanic cults will give clues to their involvement. A serious Satanist will often carry a diary. This is called a book of shadows or *Grimoire* (Moriarty & Story, 1990; Johnston, 1989). This is usually a school notebook documenting the young person's Satanic cult activity. It often serves as a notebook for other purposes, especially the doodling of cult symbols, usually pentagrams, an inverted crucifix, or a goat's head. This artwork appears to be a common activity of many youngsters preoccupied with Satanism.

Most young people who contemplate suicide as an act of homage to Satan will write about this in their book of shadows. A parent finding such a diary in the possession of an adolescent should get that person to professional help without delay. This can never be discounted as trivial, despite the protestations of the young person that it is only a game.

MAKING SENSE OF SUICIDE

For years psychologists and members of the medical profession have had difficulty explaining why a young person would act in a manner so drastic as to take his or her own life. Although theorizing is difficult, the work of Shneidman (1985) makes significant progress in understanding this problem. Basically, Shneidman proposes that suicide is an act of self-destruction that involves other people. He suggests that suicide has more to do with a relationship between two people than we previously believed. He suggests that suicide has three basic premises:

1. Suicide is an event intended to be a message from one person to another.
2. There is one specific person expected to receive the message. It is for this person that the act of suicide is committed.
3. The primary content of the message conveyed is anger.

In many cases of suicide or attempted suicide a common feature is the experience of uncontrollable levels of anger, lending greater credibility to Shneidman's theory.

For these reasons, it is important that parents address the issue of anger with their children very carefully. Whenever an adolescent begins to express thoughts of getting even with parents or makes threats to parents like "You'll be sorry for this," there should be a greater concern on the part of the parent. These types of statements are often messages that the adolescent is planning to act in some way that is self-destructive. In many cases like this the youngster is so angry and so obsessed with a need to get even or retaliate that the responsibilities for his or her own welfare are ignored. When anger escalates beyond the sense of responsibility for one's welfare, the individual is in a dangerous position.

Parents of all children, and especially of those who are troubled, should take care to ensure that their children are able to express anger verbally and feel sufficiently comfortable talking to their parents about things that make them angry. Too often parents react to a child's anger with anger of their own. This sends a message that the parent is unwilling to deal with the child's anger, or, worse yet, the child begins to feel that his or her own anger cannot be expressed without paying a high price of guilt. In either event, the only solution for a child is to bind up that anger and attempt to "ride it out." This strategy, however, never works, and a young person is left with the problem of unloading anger in ways that are inappropriate and often self-destructive.

Young people who cannot articulate their feelings of anger often pay a high price socially. The mismanagement of anger costs the teenager many friendships, often resulting in extremely limited opportunities to unload the anger. In these cases the risk factors accelerate greatly because the youngster is left only with the possibility of turning the anger toward himself or herself. Parents who allow their children the opportunity to verbally express anger and emotions in childhood will help develop a pattern of coping for the individual that will prove to be extremely helpful during adolescence.

SUICIDAL THINKING

Many parents find it frightening to hear that a great number of adolescents occasionally consider suicide. Fortunately, for the vast majority, however, they never act on those thoughts. Since suicide is so often the subject of news articles and television programs, virtually all children and adolescents have an awareness of numerous incidents of suicide before they reach young adulthood. Some people have erroneously concluded that if we refrain from talking about suicide, it will go away. Nothing could be further from the truth. A common consequence of talking about suicide is a decline in the intensity of feelings that surround it (Crespi, 1990).

When the subject of suicide is brought into a conversation with a young person, especially an adolescent, it is helpful to listen with sensitivity and to allow the individual the time to express feelings about it. Almost always, a young person who talks freely and openly about suicide and the devastation that it produces will put the act into an appropriate perspective, thereby reducing the chances that he or she will see it as a reasonable alternative to temporary problems.

A major roadblock to discussing suicide with young people is the fear it provokes in adults. Most parents are so afraid to discuss suicide that they avoid the topic altogether. When they are unable to avoid the topic, they generally convey an observable level of fear and anxiety.

When a young person brings up the subject of suicide in any discussion, the parent should respond in a calm and relaxed manner. This style of controlled talk uses a principle of reciprocal affect, used often in psychotherapy (Truax & Carkhuff, 1967). Essentially, reciprocal affect means that the level of affect or feeling in one person influences the degree of affect communicated by the other. This is also referred to as mirroring; that is, one person's body language and rate of speech often unconsciously imitates that of the other person in a conversation.

Accordingly, in a situation where a youngster is discussing suicide with any degree of agitation or anxiety, a parental response that is slow, calm, and monitored in a controlled tone of voice will allow the young-ster to begin mirroring the same speech pattern and, consequently, the emotion surrounding the topic of suicide. As a result, the individual will obtain a more realistic view of suicide and see it apart from some of the feelings and intense emotions that he or she is experiencing internally.

Finally, anger appears to be the major emotional culprit in suicidal thought as well as in Satanic interest. Parents need to provide as many opportunities as possible for their children to verbally express anger rather than allow them to hide it. Anger has a way of returning later whenever it is hidden from its real source.

CONCLUSION

In summary, when youngsters learn through experience that their par-ents are secure enough within themselves to discuss anything, especially suicide, they feel comfortable venting those feelings whenever they oc-cur in their often complicated and frustrating lives.

11

Summary

Normal and abnormal patterns of emotional development are manifest during adolescence. Ten critical elements of parenting can promote a safe and healthy transition into adulthood. These elements are helpful in guiding young people through the critical period of adolescence, and they bolster defenses against the lure of Satanism.

I have observed that adolescents who become involved in Satanic practices are strikingly similar to each other. They appear to have been deprived of these ten elements of good parenting, which represent the most effective insulation from the deceptively elusive powers of Satanism. A brief summary of them follows.

PERSONAL EMPOWERMENT

There is no question that people seek power, and adolescents are especially in need of it. Feelings of significance, authority, and personal power are the basic motives behind a number of normal behaviors shown by children and adolescents.

Anyone working with adolescents should recognize that they are highly motivated to obtain power and they will get it wherever it is made available to them. The greater their need for power, the less discretion they will use in acquiring that power. As a result, young people who feel strong needs for empowerment and are not enabled to obtain it legitimately may readily find the lure of Satanism to be an effective solution to their problems. Too often adolescents who turn to Satanic practices are driven by a pursuit of power that has been a major source of frustration in their lives for many years.

Since this need for power is formulated in the mind of a child early in life, children need opportunities that provide them with experiences of feeling independent and accomplished. The need for better problem-solving strategies for young children is an important starting point for parents to consider. We see too many young people looking to others to solve their problems. They learn from television that fantasy figures, each of whom claims a new mastery of powers over the world, solve problems through these powers. As a result, too many young children learn that the solution to difficulties is in the fantasy world of make-believe powers. This results in failure to take action in the face of troubles. Parents need to allow their children to act in order to reach effective solutions.

Young people who find Satanism especially attractive are those who look to conjured images of power to solve problems rather than taking action. Opportunities for power can be provided by giving children responsibilities, by giving them significant roles in the running of the family. They need to believe and to experience that their presence in the family makes a difference and that the family would not run well without them. Young people need to experience the same degree of involvement in community and school activities. Children who are exposed to a variety of activities in which they have meaningful participation are the least likely to see the alleged powers of Satanism as attractive. The individual who brings to the experience of adolescence strong and legitimate feelings of personal empowerment will see Satanism as ridiculous and be unaffected by it. These young people have no fear of Satanism. They recognize it for what it represents; ignorance and double-talk.

LOVE

The second most important factor for parents to consider is the development of self-esteem in childhood. Young people who enter adolescence with a strong sense of self-esteem are unlikely to look to magical power to feel better about themselves. They draw their conclusions about their self-worth from the real world, not from mystical self-deceptions. This feeling is best provided a child by parents who are able to make a clear distinction between self-esteem and the adequacy of their children's behavior. Effective discipline involves the ability to separate the doer from the deed.

In a discussion of the implications of evil in our society, Peck (1990) has concluded that the meaning of evil can only be seen in the dialectical struggle between good and evil. Within this context we can only hope that good wins out. However, if we attempt to destroy evil, we also destroy ourselves spiritually. The means to eradicate evil, then, is love: "Evil can be defeated by goodness. . . . Evil can be conquered only by love" (1990, p. 13).

All children who do something wrong or make mistakes must recognize that they are still loved and respected by their parents while being disciplined or corrected. These experiences provided in a consistent and timely manner result in a strong sense of self-esteem with the clear recognition that failing in an activity is not evidence of one's incompetence or lack of self-worth. It is simply a lesson that young people need to learn.

The sense of integrity and dignity that accompany a good self-concept are necessary prerequisites to recognizing the destructive elements contained in the philosophy of Satanism. This belief system exploits young people and promotes personal degradation, especially of women, and lacks human respect. Once this is openly recognized, Satanism becomes repulsive rather than attractive.

AN ACCURATE ASSESSMENT OF EVIL

Children need to learn at an early age that there are evil people in the world. While some parents would like their children to believe that everyone is bad and no one can be trusted, this style of parenting leaves the child with a sense of insecurity, a lack of trust, and in more serious cases, elements of paranoid thought patterns. This youngster is suspicious of everyone and unlikely to venture into the world feeling safe or secure.

On the other hand, some parents would like their children to believe that everyone is good and trustworthy. These children often find themselves relating to the world in a manner that is naive and so trusting of others that they often become victims of manipulation. A middle ground between these extremes is more appropriate for raising children.

Young people must recognize that some people can be trusted, loved, and respected but only those who give evidence of worthy intentions.

These young people learn to perceptively evaluate the motives of strangers and take care not to entrust them with their personal safety.

In addition to personal security around trusted people, a child also needs to learn that some people are evil and must be avoided and cannot be trusted. This discussion of evil can be better understood if we divide it into two types, evil by design and evil by default. Some people, I believe, are evil by design. They actively pursue their evil activity, and our interventions are very limited, usually resulting in failure. Examples of people evil by design are drug pushers, child molesters, pimps, and child pornographers. Also, some are Satanists, like the Psychopathic Delinquents described in Chapter 2. These people should be avoided.

Another type is evil by default. This individual stumbles into activity out of neglect, dependence, and the refusal to take responsibility for his or her emotional needs. They rarely set out to be evil. They just fall into it. Many of these people are Satanic cult dabblers. They are drawn to Satanism to fill a void, because no relationship or direction was given to them when they were most needy and vulnerable. They suffer from a twofold problem: the lack of direction in their lives and the lack of proper relations. This is the evil described by Friedman (1990). It is the result of estrangement from others and a failure to find meaningful direction in life. These people can and should be helped. We can provide these young people with relationships and direction if we are not afraid to do so. Our fear of these people is simply a matter of our own misunderstanding and ignorance.

A healthy child should have an accurate perception of the balance between good and evil in the world and routinely acknowledge the need for corresponding behavior appropriate for dealing with certain people. We cannot eradicate evil in the world, but we can routinely avoid it.

RELIGION

If children are raised in an environment that teaches them that God is good, they see God as a source of security, consolation, concern, care, and unconditional love. Some parents, however, often resort to religion as a means of keeping their children in line. The result of this upbringing is a view of God as a bad guy, one who is there to remind children of their imperfections and weaknesses. What results from this view of God is clearly not in the mental health interests of the child. The child's mind begins to associate the presence of God too closely with internal feelings of guilt. As children's guilt builds over time and becomes more sharply defined in adolescence, it is likely that they will also conclude that to get away from guilt they must get away from God. Once this conclusion is reached, it becomes necessary to abandon the idea of God in order to avoid guilt. Once the concept of God is rejected, a void results, waiting to be filled by another mystical system. The system of choice for some is the antithesis of God, Satan.

Problems associated with the adolescent's guilt management are especially difficult for parents. On one hand, guilt is a powerful motivator used by many parents to obtain complaint behavior from a child. A young child given the choice between being good and going to hell will probably choose to be good, for a while, at least. This strategy works so well with some children that parents tend to rely on manipulating guilt too frequently in their attempts to train children to behave themselves. Using this guilt management strategy to promote good religious behavior on the part of the child is risky and can lead to other problems.

When guilt levels become out of proportion to their psychological function, there is an intense need to move away from those feelings. When guilt feelings are so entwined with one's religion, it is predictable that adolescents may reject their religious beliefs because they cannot separate them from guilt. The need for relief from guilt causes the only practical solution to be the rejection of the religion.

DRUG AND ALCOHOL USE

Adolescents who find Satanism attractive are in an extremely high risk category for drug and alcohol abuse. In fact, many law enforcement people believe that the proliferation of drugs is highly associated with the rise of interest in Satanism (Story, 1987). Some young people report their initial involvement in cult activities is facilitated through the use of drugs. In addition, there are many reports of adolescents invited to drug parties where they are first exposed to Satanism. Most therapists working with adolescents involved in Satanic practices also report that their clients have associated drug problems.

Parents concerned about the proper emotional development of their children need to follow the current principles of education for the prevention of drug use and abuse by providing good supervision and alternative ways of having fun. In addition, parents need to pay special attention to their own attitudes about drugs and alcohol and the inherent problems that result from their use. Observing parent drug and alcohol use is the first exposure children have to this problem. This is especially important for parents of younger children. Children acquire attitudes about drugs and alcohol much earlier in life than we previously had believed.

PRIVACY

A common complaint of parents is the unreasonable demand for privacy by their rebellious adolescents. Parents who are afraid to confront their adolescents with strong management strategies often concede to these demands. Parental ignorance inadvertently aggravates a great deal of adolescent misbehavior. This is no more evident than in the area of Satanic cult activities. Many young Satanists will have a variety of signs and symbols in their rooms that are indicators of their involvement in Satanic practice. Their demands for rights to privacy, however, have kept parents ignorant of what goes on in their own house.

Parents should allow as much privacy as can be responsibly maintained. However, all parents, as long as they pay the rent or mortgage, should maintain the right of access to their children's bedrooms. If a child learns early that personal privacy is related to their level of responsibility, he or she will routinely accept the idea that privacy is obtained by acting in an appropriate manner.

KNOWLEDGE

Knowledge is power. Parents need a rational understanding of the elements of Satanism if they are to effectively combat its influence. Much of the mysticism of Satanism is facilitated by the ignorance of parents. Parents who are able to freely discuss issues of strong emotional significance with their children will maintain the influence necessary to protect their adolescents from negative influences as well. This openness and knowledge is not restricted to Satanism but should also include sexuality, drug abuse, and peer relationships and the influence that they bring to bear on the daily life of an adolescent.

HELPING OTHERS

There are few experiences in life more powerfully rewarding than the personal satisfaction of being helpful to another person, especially in times of great personal need. A child needs to learn as early as possible the value and worth of activities that are genuinely altruistic. The experience of helping another individual lends a sense of dignity and a bond between a child and another person. In addition, it fosters a sense of significance and the feeling that an individual can make a difference in the world. This feeling is a great source of personal power and needs to be nurtured.

Too often parents are lacking in their support in these activities for their children because they are inclined to see their children as too young or the activity too inconvenient for the parents' schedule, or they simply fail to recognize the significance of these activities for children. Taking on roles at home that help in running the house and helping neighbors and old people are a few examples of what young children can do. Adolescents can expand into the world with the same sense of altruism, making time to help others.

COMMUNICATION

Parents of healthy children are good communicators. They are willing to extend their energy in the direction of expressing themselves to their children and giving children the opportunities to express themselves in return. It is especially important that communication about matters pertaining to anger, especially during adolescence, be given a high priority in the family. In addition, it is equally important to be able to discuss openly those things which are potential sources of guilt for a child.

Open communications with their parents gives adolescents a sense of emotional support. Too often adolescents who become troubled or entangled in problems with peers are inclined to move away from parents rather than toward them. This tendency has its roots in childhood experiences when parents have not been available to the child in times of distress. Parents who do not recognize the significance of communicating with children around a variety of emotional issues are more likely to experience personal alienation from their children during adolescence.

ROLE MODELS

Parents often fail to recognize the importance of their own personal behavior and conduct in the mind of a child or adolescent. Parents who serve as good role models by showing their children how to solve problems and how to be responsible to themselves and others are providing experiences of profound significance to the emotional well-being of the child. Parents who are cheerful, positive, and good-humored are most likely to raise children who are able to see things from a rational perspective. Positive attitudes and an enthusiasm for life aid the development of children and help insulate them from negative influences.

Parents sometimes role model double standards. They will demand honesty from their children but brag about cheating on taxes or getting away with something illegal. Other parents will demand strict adherence to religious standards but violate these practices in their own behavior. Adolescents who begin to experience a period of rebelliousness will likely reject the parent who models double standards. Unfortunately, a rebellious adolescent may also reject the positive standards practiced by the parent. In many cases we see the rejection of family religious practices justified by parental double standards of personal practice. A rebellious adolescent who succeeds in rejecting parents and their religious background is rendered more vulnerable to the alternative presented by Satanism.

CONCLUSION

Parenting is filled with pitfalls. With a good dose of common sense and recognition of the emotional aspects of the adolescent experience, however, this difficult and at times totally exasperating phase will pass with time. It may not be easy, but it is worth the effort.

References

Abramson, L. Y., Seligman, M. E. P., & Teasdale, J. D. (1978). Learned helplessness in humans: Critique and reformulation. *Journal of Abnormal Psychology, 87,* 49–74.

Allberg, W. R., & Chu, L. (1990). Understanding adolescent suicide: Correlates in a developmental perspective. *The School Counselor, 37*(5), 343–350.

American Psychiatric Association. (1987). *Diagnostic and statistical manual of mental disorders: Third edition-Revised.* Washington, D.C.: American Psychiatric Association Press.

Anderson, J. (1988, April 18). Satanic crime: Police say the devil made some people do it. *Chicago Tribune* (Tempo), p. 1.

Ashley, L. R. N. (1988). *The amazing world of superstition, prophecy, luck, magic and witchcraft.* New York: Bell.

Balducci, C. (1990). *The Devil: Alive and active in our world* (J. Aumann, Trans.) New York: Alba House Press.

Bandura, A. (1973). *Aggression: A social learning analysis.* Englewood Cliffs, NJ: Prentice-Hall.

Bar-Joseph, H., & Tzuriel, D. (1990). Suicidal tendencies and ego identity in adolescence. *Adolescence, 25*(97), 215–223.

Baron, R. A. (1985). Aggression. In H. I. Kaplan & B. J. Sadock (Eds.), *Comprehensive textbook of psychiatry: IV.* Baltimore, MD: Williams and Wilkins, 213–225.

Baumeister, R. F. (1990). Suicide as escape from self. *Psychological Review, 97*(1), 90–113.

Blos, P. (1962). *On adolescence*. New York: Free Press.

Bourget, D., Gagnon, A., & Bradford, J. M. (1988). Satanism in a psychiatric adolescent population. *Canadian Journal of Psychiatry, 33*(3), 197–202.

Burns, T., & Laughlin, Jr., C. D. (1979). Ritual and social power. In E. G. d'Aquili, C. D. Laughlin, Jr., & J. McManus (Eds.), *The spectrum of ritual: A biogenetic structural analysis*. New York: Columbia University Press, 249–279.

California Office of Criminal Justice Planning. (1990). *Occult crime: A law enforcement primer. Research update: Special edition*. Sacramento, CA.

Cameron, N. (1963). *Personality development and psychopathology: A dynamic approach*. Boston: Houghton Mifflin.

Campbell, J. (1988). *The power of myth*. New York: Doubleday.

Carlson, R., & Shield, B. (Eds.). (1989). *Healers on healing*. Los Angeles: Jeremy Tarcher.

Carlson, S., & Larue, G. (1989). *Satanism in America: How the devil got much more than his due*. El Cerrito, CA: Gaia Press.

Combs, A. W., & Snygg, D. (1959). *Individual behavior: A perceptual approach to behavior*. New York: Harper and Row.

Conway, F., & Siegleman, J. (1979). *Snapping: America's epidemic of sudden personality change*. New York: Dell.

Crabtree, A. (1985). *Multiple man: Explorations in possession and multiple personality*. New York: Praeger.

Crespi, T. D. (1990). Approaching adolescent suicide: Queries and signposts. *The School Counselor, 37*(4), 256–260.

Cunningham, S. (1988). *The truth about witchcraft today*. St. Paul, MN: Llewellyn Press.

Davis, P. (1983). *Suicidal adolescents*. Springfield, IL: Charles C. Thomas.

Davis, W. (1985). *The serpent and the rainbow*. New York: Simon and Schuster.

Drury, N. (1989). *The occult experience: Magic in the new age*. Garden City Park, NY: Avery.

Erikson, E. H. (1968). *Identity: Youth and crisis*. New York: Norton.

Fowler, R. C., Rich, C. L., & Young, D. (1986). San Diego suicide study II: Substance abuse in young cases. *Archives of General Psychiatry, 43*, 962–965.

Fox, J. J. (1989). Category and complement: Binary ideologies and the organization of dualism in Eastern Indonesia. In D. Maybury-Lewis & U. Almagor (Eds.), 33–56. *The attraction of opposites: Thought and society in the dualistic mode*. Ann Arbor: University of Michigan Press.

Friedman, M. (1990). The human dimension of evil. *The Journal of Pastoral Counseling, 25*(1), 26–36.

Fromm, E. (1973). *The anatomy of human destructiveness*. New York: Holt, Rinehart and Winston.

Galanter, M. (1989). *Cults: Faith healing and coercion.* New York: Oxford University Press.

Gold, M., & Petrino, R. J. (1980). Delinquent behavior in adolescence. In J. Adelson (Ed.), *Handbook of Adolescent Psychology.* New York: Wiley, 495–535.

Goldsmith, D. F., & Clark, E. (1987). Children and moving. In A. Thomas & J. Grimes (Eds.) *Children's needs: Psychological perspectives.* Washington, DC: National Association of School Psychologists, 372–378.

Gray, W. (1989). *Between good and evil: Polarities of power.* St. Paul, MN: Llewellyn Press.

Haizlip, T. M., Corder, B. F., & Ball, B. C. (1984). The adolescent murderer. In C. R. Keith (Ed.), *The aggressive adolescent: Clinical perspectives.* New York: Free Press, 126–148.

Helmstetter, S. (1986). *What to say when you talk to yourself.* New York: Pocket Books.

Hendlin, R. (1985). Suicide among the young: Psychodynamics and demography. In M. L. Peck, N. L. Farberow, & R. E. Litman (Eds.), *Youth suicide.* New York: Springer, 19–38.

Hicks, R. D. (1991). *In pursuit of Satan: The police and the occult.* Buffalo, NY: Promethius Books.

Hill, D., & Williams, P. (1965). *The supernatural.* New York: Hawthorn Books.

Hinsie, L. E., & Campbell, R. J. (1974). *Psychiatric Dictionary* (4th ed.). New York: Oxford University Press.

Holmes, R. M. (1989, Fall). Youth in the occult: A model of Satanic involvement. *The National FOP Journal,* pp. 20–22.

Imber-Black, E., Roberts, J., & Whiting, R. (Eds.). (1988). *Rituals in families and family therapy.* New York: Norton.

Johanson, G., & Kurtz, R. (1991). Grace unfolding: Psychotherapy and the Tao-te-Ching. *Common Boundary, 9*(3), 22–26.

Johnston, J. (1989). *The edge of evil: The rise of Satanism in North America.* Dallas: Word.

Jung, C. G. (1959). *Aion: Researches into the phenomenology of the self* (R. F. C. Hull, Trans.). Princeton, NJ: Princeton University Press.

Jung, C. G. (1971). *The portable Jung* (R. F. C. Hull, Trans.). New York: Viking.

Jung, C. G. (1973). *Boundaries of the soul* (J. Singer, Ed.). New York: Anchor.

Kaczmarek, B. L., & Backlund, B. A. (1991). Disenfranchised grief: The loss of an adolescent relationship. *Adolescence, 26*(102), 469–475.

Kahaner, L. (1988). *Cults that kill.* New York: Warner.

Kekes, J. (1988). Understanding evil. *American Philosophical Quarterly, 25*(1), 13–24.

Koestenbaum, R. (1971). *The vitality of death.* Westport, CT: Greenwood.

Lamb, M. E. (Ed.). (1981). *The role of the father in child development* (2nd ed.). New York: Wiley.

Lanning, K. V. (1989, October). Satanic, occult, ritualistic crime: A law enforcement perspective. *Police Chief,* pp. 62–83.

LaVey, A. S. (1969). *The Satanic bible.* New York: Avon.

Lefevre, P. (1989, November 24). Catholics most vulnerable to cults: Sects and Satanism stir church to action. *The National Catholic Reporter,* 2.

Lester, D. (1988). *Suicide from a psychological perspective.* Springfield, IL: Charles C. Thomas.

Litman, R. E., & Diller, J. (1985). Case studies in youth suicide. In M. L. Peck, N. L. Farberow, & R. E. Litman (Eds.), *Youth suicide.* New York: Springer, 48–70.

Lyons, A. (1988). *Satan wants you: The cult of devil worship in America.* New York: The Mysterious Press.

MacHovec, F. J. (1989). *Cults and personality.* Springfield, IL: Charles C. Thomas.

Maris, R. (1985). The suicide problem. *Suicide and Life-Threatening Behavior, 15,* 91–109.

Maslow, A. H. (1969). *The psychology of science: A reconnaissance.* Chicago: Henry Regnery.

Masterson, J. F. (1985). *Treatment of the borderline adolescent: A developmental approach.* New York: Brunner-Mazel.

May, R., Angel, E., & Ellenberger, H. F. (1958). *Existence: A new dimension in psychiatry and psychology.* New York: Simon and Schuster.

Maybury-Lewis, D., & Almagor, U. (Eds.). (1989). *The attraction of opposites: Thought and society in the dualistic mode.* Ann Arbor: University of Michigan Press.

Millon, T. (1981). *Disorders of personality: DSM III: Axis II.* New York: Wiley.

Montagu, A. (1950). *On being human.* New York: Hawthorn Books.

Moriarty, A. R., & Story, D. W. (1990). Psychological dynamics of adolescent Satanism. *Journal of Mental Health Counseling, 12*(2), 186–198.

Murphy, S. J., G. R. (1979). A ceremonial ritual: The mass. In E. G. d'Aquili, C. D. Laughlin, Jr., & J. McManus (Eds.), *The spectrum of ritual: A biogenetic structural analysis.* New York: Columbia University Press, 318–341.

Myerhoff, B. (1982). Rites of passage: Process and paradox. In V. Turner (Ed.), *Celebration: Studies in festivity and ritual.* Washington, DC: Smithsonian Institution.

Naisbitt, J. (1984). *Megatrends: Ten new directions transforming our lives.* New York: Warner Books.

Neiger, B. L., & Hopkins, R. W. (1988). Adolescent suicide: Character traits of high risk teenagers. *Adolescence, 23*(90), 469–475.

Paci, S. (1990, December). Satan the great activist. *30 Days,* 50–53.

Parents' Music Resource Center. (1986). *Let's talk rock: A primer for parents.* Arlington, VA: Parents' Music Resource Center Press.

Patterson, C. H. (1986). *Theories of counseling and psychotherapy* (4th ed.). New York: Harper and Row.

Peck, M. S. (1990). Reflections on the psychology of evil. *The Journal of Pastoral Counseling, 25*(1), 8–14.

Pulling, P. (1989). *The devil's web.* Richmond, VA: B.A.D.D. Press.

Quay, H. C. (1987). Patterns of delinquent behavior. In H. C. Quay (Ed.), *Handbook of juvenile delinquency.* New York: Wiley, 118–138.

Raschke, C. A. (1990). *Painted black.* San Francisco: Harper and Row.

Rich, C. L., et al. (1986). San Diego suicide study: Comparison of gay to straight males. *Suicide and Life-Threatening Behavior, 16,* 448–457.

Roberts, J. (1988). Setting the frame: Definition, functions, and typology of rituals. In E. Imber-Black, J. Roberts, & R. Whiting (Eds.), *Rituals in families and family therapy.* New York: Norton, 3–47.

Rotheram-Borus, M. J., et al. (1990). Cognitive style and pleasant activities among female adolescent suicide attempters. *Journal of Consulting and Clinical Psychology, 58*(5), 554–561.

Russell, B. (1945). *A history of western philosophy.* New York: Simon and Schuster.

Russell, J. B. (1988). *The prince of darkness: Radical evil and the power of good in human history.* New York: Cornell University Press.

Sangree, W. H. (1971). Twinship and the premise of ambiguity: Leadership, witchcraft, and disease in Irigwe, Nigeria. *L'Homme, 11*(3), 64–70.

Seligman, M. E. P. (1975). *Helplessness: On depression, development, and death.* San Francisco: Freeman Press.

Shneidman, E. (1985). *Definition of suicide.* New York: Wiley.

Siegel, B. S. (1990). *Peace, love, and healing.* New York: Harper and Row.

Simandl, R. J., & Naysmith, B. (1988, August). Dabbling their way to ritual crime. *Cult Awareness Network News,* p. 4.

Sorrel, W. E. (1978). Cults and cult suicide. *International Journal of Group Tensions, 8*(3–4), 96–105.

St. Clair, D. (1987). *Say you love Satan.* New York: Dell.

Stackpole, M. A. (1989). The truth about role playing games. In S. Carlson & G. Larue (Eds.), *Satanism in America: How the devil got more than his due.* El Cerrito, CA: Gaia Press.

Story, D. W. (1987, September). Ritualistic crime: A new challenge to law enforcement. *Law and Order,* pp. 81–83.

Strang, S. P., & Orlofsky, J. L. (1990). Factors underlying suicidal ideation among college students: A test of Teicher and Jacobs' model. *Journal of Adolescence, 13*(1), 39–52.

Thetford, W. N., & Walsh, R. (1985). Theories of personality and psychopathology: Schools derived from philosophy and psychology. In H. I. Kaplan & B. J. Sadock (Eds.), *Comprehensive textbook of psychiatry* (4th ed.). Baltimore: Williams and Wilkins.

Truax, C. B., & Carkhuff, R. R. (1967). *Toward effective counseling and psychotherapy: Training and practice*. Chicago: Aldine.

Turner, V. (Ed.). (1982). *Celebration: Studies in festivity and ritual*. Washington, DC: Smithsonian Institution.

Valle, R. S. (1989). The emergence of transpersonal psychology. In R. S. Valle & S. Halling (Eds.), *Existential-phenomenological perspectives in psychology*. New York: Plenum Press, 257–268.

van Gennep, A. (1960). *The rites of passage* (M. B. Vizedom & G. L. Caffee, Trans.). Chicago: University of Chicago Press.

Wheeler, B. R., Wood, S., & Hatch, R. J. (1988). Assessment and intervention with adolescents involved in Satanism. *Social Work, 33*(6), 547–550.

White, B. (1985). *The first three years of life*. Englewood Cliffs, NJ: Prentice-Hall.

Wolpe, J. (1958). *Psychotherapy by reciprocal inhibition*. Stanford, CA: Stanford University Press.

Wood, C. (1987, March 30). Suicide and Satanism. *MacLean's: Canada's Weekly Newsmagazine,* p. 54.

Yengoyan, A. A. (1989). Language and conceptual dualism: Sacred and secular concepts in Australian aboriginal cosmology and myth. In D. Maybury-Lewis & U. Almagor (Eds.), *The attraction of opposites: Thought and society in the dualistic mode*. Ann Arbor: University of Michigan Press, 171–190.

Author Index

Abramson, L., 117, 135
Allberg, W., 112, 113, 114, 135
Almagor, U., 55, 136, 138, 140
Anderson, J., 13, 122, 135
Angel, E., 56, 111, 120, 138
Ashley, L., 106, 135

Backlund, B., 117, 137
Balducci, C., 57, 58, 135
Ball, B., 83, 137
Bandura, A., 40, 135
Bar-Joseph, H., 117, 135
Baron, R., 40, 135
Baumeister, R., 117, 135
Blenbush, J., 121
Blos, P., 122, 136
Bourget, D., 12, 114, 136
Bradford, J., 12, 114, 136
Burns, T., 65, 136

Cameron, N., 57, 67, 136
Campbell, J., 66–69, 136

Campbell, R., 67, 137
Carkhuff, R., 125, 140
Carlson, R., 109, 136
Carlson, S., 77, 105, 136, 139
Chu, L., 112, 113, 114, 135
Clark, E., 24, 137
Cloward, R., 48
Combs, A., 60, 114, 136
Conway, F., 6, 77, 121, 136
Corder, B., 83, 137
Crabtree, A., 9, 136
Crespi, T., 125, 136
Cunningham, S., 7, 136

d'Aquili, E., 136, 138
Davis, P., 118, 136
Davis, W., 8, 136
Diller, J., 115, 138
Drury, N., 73, 136

Ellenberger, H., 56, 111, 120, 138
Erikson, E., 70, 136

Farberow, N., 137, 138
Fowler, R., 112, 121, 136
Fox, J., 55, 136
Friedman, M., 130, 136
Fromm, E., 109, 136

Gagnon, A., 12, 114, 136
Galanter, M., 6, 83, 137
Gold, M., 48, 137
Goldsmith, D., 24, 137
Gray, W., 57, 137
Grimes, J., 137

Haizlip, T., 83, 137
Halling, S., 140
Hatch, R., 11, 12, 140
Helmstetter, S., 31, 137
Hendlin, R., 113, 117, 137
Hicks, R., 106, 137
Hill, D., 7, 137
Hinsie, L., 67, 137
Holmes, R., 11, 137
Hopkins, R., 112, 138
Horton, R., 64

Imber-Black, E., 66, 68, 137, 139

Johanson, G., 109, 137
Johnston, J., 4, 20, 121, 123, 137
Jung, C., 57, 58, 120, 137

Kaczmarek, B., 117, 137
Kahaner, L., 3, 137
Kaplan, H., 135, 139
Kekes, J., 57, 137
Koestenbaum, R., 56, 69, 120, 137
Kurtz, R., 109, 137

Lamb, M., 68, 138
Lanning, K., 11, 138
Larue, G., 77, 105, 136, 139

Laughlin, C., 65, 136
LaVey, A., 5, 10, 11, 37–45, 59,
    68, 108, 115, 117, 118, 138
LeBar, J., 64
Lefevre, P., 64, 138
Lester, D., 116, 138
Litman, R., 115, 137, 138
Lyons, A., 3, 14, 20, 138

MacHovec, F., 6, 138
McManus, J., 136, 138
Maris, R., 112, 138
Maslow, A., 109, 138
Masterson, J., 47, 138
May, R., 56, 111, 120, 138
Maybury-Lewis, D., 55, 136, 138,
    140
Millon, T., 15, 138
Montagu, A., 40, 138
Moriarty, A., 11, 12, 62, 123, 138
Murphy, G., 64, 138
Murray, H., 47
Myerhoff, B., 64, 65, 68, 74, 138

Naisbitt, J., 112, 138
Naysmith, B., 11, 12, 139
Neiger, B., 112, 138

Ohlin, L., 48
Orlofsky, J., 118, 139

Paci, S., 58, 138
Patterson, C. H., 73, 139
Peck, M. L., 137, 138
Peck, M. S., 129, 139
Petrino, R., 48, 137
Pulling, P., 4, 139

Quay, H., 14, 139

Raschke, C., 4, 139
Rich, C., 112, 121, 136, 139
Roberts, J., 65, 66, 68, 137, 139
Rotheram-Borus, M., 118, 139
Russell, B., 56, 139
Russell, J. B., 57, 58, 139

Sadock, B., 135, 140
St. Clair, D., 3, 139
Sangree, W. H., 55, 139
Seligman, M., 50, 98, 117, 135, 139
Shield, B., 109, 136
Shneidman, E., 20, 119, 123, 124, 139
Siegel, B., 109, 139
Siegleman, J., 6, 77, 121, 136
Simandl, R., 11, 12, 139
Snygg, D., 60, 114, 136
Sorrel, W., 122, 139
Stackpole, M., 4, 139
Story, D., 11, 12, 62, 123, 131, 138, 139
Strang, S., 118, 139

Teasdale, J., 117, 135
Thetford, W., 47, 139
Thomas, A., 137
Truax, C., 125, 140
Turner, V., 65, 138, 140
Tzuriel, D., 117, 135

Valle, R., 109, 140
Van Gennep, A., 69, 140

Walsh, R., 47, 139
Wheeler, B., 11, 12, 140
White, B., 82–83, 140
Whiting, R., 66, 68, 137, 139
Williams, P., 8, 137
Wolpe, J., 87, 140
Wood, C., 122, 140
Wood, S., 11, 12

Yengoyan, A., 55, 56, 140
Young, D., 112, 121, 136

Subject Index

aboriginal culture, 55

academic demands, 25, 73

advertising, 72, 74

aggression, 17, 40

aggressive needs, 17

AIDS (Acquired Immune Deficiency Syndrome), 24, 65

alcohol, 67, 81, 112, 120, 121, 131; alcohol problems, 21

alienation, 2, 47, 113

American Psychiatric Association, 14, 18, 19

amotivational syndrome, 29

anger, 5, 16, 32, 40, 47, 124; free floating, 118

Angry Misfit (personality type), 13, 15–17, 118

anonymous friends, 35

anthropology, 3, 55

Antichrist, 58, 120

antisocial personality disorder, 19

anxiety, 24, 32; hidden, 100

astrology, 48

baptism, 64

Batman, 51

Black Mass, 108

black witches, 7

blocked opportunity, 48

body-mind balance, 66, 109

body weight, 26

bonding, 33

Bothered About Dungeons and Dragons (BADD), 4

Brujeria, 8

bully, 47, 92

California Office of Criminal Justice Planning, 8

candles, 14

Cathars, 57

catharsis, 88

Catholic church, 8, 58; Mass, 64

Christianity, 38, 41, 58, 62, 64

clothing styles, 27

cognitive dissonance, 79

commitment, 74

common ground, 108
communication, 3, 95–110, 133; in
  crises, 95, 101–5
confabulation, 89
confirmation rites, 64
conflict management, 26
conspiracy theory, 4
cooperative behavior, 40
counterphobic behavior, 67
criminal activity, 14
critical thinking, 18, 105
crusades, 58
cultural risk factors, 23
curfew, 85

dabbling, 12, 20
death, 66; acceptance of, 69
deception, 53
defense mechanisms, 88
definition game, 101
demonic possession, 58
denial, 79, 81, 119
dependency, 16, 33, 45, 92, 122
depression, 32, 47, 117
developmental tasks, 12, 70
diagnosis, 13
dialectical idealism, 55
dichotomous thinking, 29, 61
discipline, 83, 129
disillusionment, 47
domination, 14
double binds, 85, 92, 96, 115
drugs, 14, 21, 24, 26, 29, 65, 67,
  81, 112, 120, 131
dual diagnosis, 20
dualities, 55–62; and death, 56, 111;
  and evil, 57; of heaven and hell,
  59; in language, 56; in philosophy,
  55
Dungeons and Dragons, 3, 5

Eastern mysticism, 109
education, 74
emancipation, 70, 72, 74
empathy, 96
empowerment, 127
emptiness, 47
Enochian Keys, 42
escapism, 67
estrangement, 73
evil, 4, 5, 7, 58, 59, 129; by default,
  130; by design, 130
exorcism, 58
experts, 63
exposure to problems, 103

family: anchors, 24, 113; rituals, 74,
  104; routines, 34; values, 3
father, role in development, 68
fear, 3, 5, 47, 60, 66
feeling, responding to, 88
football, 47
forever statements, 98
forgiveness, 26
Freud, S., 52
friendships, 35
fundamentalism, 2
funeral rites, 69
future, 42, 117
futurists, 25, 112

Gestalt therapy, 73
grandiosity, 18
Grimoire, 123
guilt, 33, 41, 45, 47, 86, 88, 102,
  115, 130

habits, 26
Haitian culture, 8
Hegel, G. W., 55
helping others, 132
helplessness, 2, 31, 47, 50, 52, 98,

104; as learned behavior, 50, 98, 102, 116–17
hidden anxieties, 100
horoscopes, 48
hospitalization, 19
hostility, 17, 33
human sacrifice, 4
humor, 105

illnesses, 27
impulsiveness, 28, 29, 32, 114, 115, 118
incarceration, 14
independence, 60
independence training, 81
Indonesian culture, 55
innate aggression, 40
inquisitions, 58
insecurity, 38
interpersonal relationships, 26
intervention plan, 13
inverted cross, 27
Irigwe tribe, 55

Jones, Rev. Jim, 121, 122
Jonestown, 121
Judeo-Christian, 7

Knights of Columbus, 65
knowledge, 18, 107, 132

language development, 83
last rites, 64
law enforcement, 14
leadership, 82
learned aggression, 40
LeBar, Fr. James, 64
life: complexity of, 23, 112; transitions, 71
limits: setting, 83; testing, 84, 85
love, 128

"love bombing," 83
Lucifer, 57

Manicheans, 57
marriage, 64, 65
Marx, K., 56
masochism, 39
Masons, 65
masturbation, 43
Metamoros, Mexico, 107
Michael the Archangel, 58
mirroring, 125
missed attribution, 98
money habits, 35
motivation, 29
multigenerational cult families, 9, 13
multiple personality disorders, 9, 13
music, 16, 27, 34, 72; heavy metal, 16
mysticism, 20, 71, 73, 108, 109

narcissism, 75; primary, 52
narcissistic personality disorder, 18
National Catholic Reporter, 64
Necronomicon, 105–6
negative reinforcement, 59
new age movement, 109
Nigeria, 8

occult, 39
oppositional behavior, 15, 58, 60, 99, 111
oppositional defiant disorder, 15
Ouija Boards, 48
ownership of problems, 102

Palo Mayombe, 8
parallel communications, 97
parallel lifestyles, 78
Parents' Music Resource Center (PMRC), 5

parenting, 77–94; problems of, 79–
    80, 83, 92
parent unavailability, 25
passivity, 50
peer: groups, 16; pressure, 26, 114
pentagram, 27
perceived loss, 117
perceptual power, 49
perceptual stress, 30
perceptual threat, 28, 99, 114
personality types, 11–21
philosophy, 3
physical risk factors, 26
power, 2, 14, 41, 44, 45, 47–59,
    71, 107; as illusion, 49; develop-
    mental considerations of, 51
powerlessness, 51, 53
praise, 83, 86
prayer, 113
presenting problem, 21
privacy, 34, 132
private meanings, 95
Pseudo-Intellectual (personality type),
    13, 17–19
psychiatric horsemen of the Apoca-
    lypse, 47
psychic tension, 62
psychological anchoring, 68, 71, 104
psychological autopsies, 115
psychological defenses, 27
psychological risk factors, 28
Psychopathic Delinquent (personality
    type), 13, 14–15
psychopathology, 6, 9
psychotherapy, 73, 109, 125; training
    for, 74
punishment, 91

quality time, 104
questioning, 107

reactive courage, 67
reciprocal affect, 125
reciprocal inhibition, 87
rejection, 26; of religion, 61
relatedness, 109
religion, 3, 38, 44, 91, 130; as an-
    chor, 113; and cults, 6, 7, 77,
    121–22; and suicide, 119; and to-
    talitarianism, 4; training, 6
respect, 96
responsibilities, 80, 103
reversal of good and bad, 41
reversed feelings, 33
rights, 80
rigidity in thinking, 28
risk factors, 23–36
rites of passage, 63–75
ritual, 64, 108; countercultural, 71;
    family, 104
role of the father, 68
role models, 24, 33, 90–91, 103,
    134
rootedness, 24, 109
rules of conduct, 68

sacraments, 64
sadistic personality disorder, 14
Santeria, 8
Satanic Bible, 2, 37–45, 59, 61, 68
Satanic folklore, 105
scare tactics, 4
science, 73
secrecy, 30, 44, 53
self-actualization, 109
self-blame, 102
self-concept, 30–32
self-disclosure, 89
self-esteem, 2, 86, 116, 128
self-exploration, 18
self-help groups, 15

self-talk, 31, 116
sex, 43; adolescent, 24, 67, 115;
    drive, 38, 44
single parents, 93
slave trade, 8
sleep habits, 27; disturbance, 27
social risk factors, 34
Socrates, 56
Socratic method, 56
spontaneous remission, 32
street gangs, 24, 47, 48, 51, 65
stress, 61; management, 30
subliminal perception, 5
suicidal ambivalence, 123
suicidal ideation, 19, 53
Suicidal Impulsive (personality type),
    13, 19–21
suicidal rituals, 20
suicide, 2, 32, 65, 67, 69, 111–26;
    dyadic theory of, 124; pacts, 20;
    rates, 112; risk assessment, 20
Superman, 51
symptom, Satanism as, 6, 13, 43
symptom suppression, 11, 13

tarot, 48
telekinesis, 107

television, 24, 83
termination issues, 16
theology, 38
time perspective, 24, 114
transcendence, 109
transcending fear, 67
transitions in life, 65, 71
truth, 18, 106

undersocialized aggressive personal-
    ity, 14

vague messages, 100
values, rejection of, 61
vicarious satisfaction, 15
violence, 14, 40
volunteerism, 75
voodoo, 8
voudons, 8
vulnerability, 38, 78

weakness, 39
weapons, 51
werewolves, 107
witchcraft, 7

ABOUT THE AUTHOR

ANTHONY MORIARTY is a Licensed Clinical Psychologist who has been in private practice since 1980. He is also Assistant Principal at Rich Township High School in Illinois, and has written for the *Journal of Mental Health Counseling, Social Work in Education,* and various law enforcement journals.

Woltermann